# Celtic, Medieval and Tudor Wall Hangings in 1/12 Scale Needlepoint

Stone slab showing typical Celtic designs; Aberlemno, Tayside, Scotland

# Celtic, Medieval and Tudor Wall Hangings in 1/12 Scale Needlepoint

## SANDRA WHITEHEAD

**Guild of Master Craftsman Publications Ltd**

First published 2000
by Guild of Master Craftsman Publications Ltd
Castle Place, 166 High Street, Lewes
East Sussex BN7 1XU

Reprinted 2001

A catalogue record for this book is available from the British Library.

ISBN 1 86108 181 2

Designed and edited by Christopher and Gail Lawther
Cover design by Ian Smith at GMC Publications design studio
Set in Utopia and Gill Sans
Colour origination by Viscan Graphics (Singapore)
Printed in China by Sun Fung Offset Binding Co. Ltd.

# Contents

## Measurements

Although care has been taken to ensure that imperial measurements are true and accurate, they are only conversions from metric; they have been rounded up or down to the nearest $1/8$in, or to the nearest convenient equivalent in cases where the metric measurements themselves are only approximate.

Care should therefore be taken to use either imperial or metric measurements consistently. The exact size of the finished designs is dependent on the stitch count and the gauge of the canvas used.

# Preparing to Stitch

*Left:* craftsmen working on embroidered hangings, shown in an Italian manuscript dated around 1400.

*Right:* women involved in preparing fibres, spinning and weaving, from a French manuscript

# Introduction

MY ENTHUSIASM for Celtic, medieval and Tudor designs has been with me for as long as I can remember. My favourite lessons at school included craft and history – although my memory for dates was dreadful! Modern history didn't hold the same appeal for me as the study of earlier periods, and I found myself drawn to medieval and Tudor times in particular.

My interest continued to grow over the years, and I've built up quite a library of history, art and needlecraft books; my favourite books have always been those on historical needlework. I love to design historical costumes in miniature, and a few years ago I bought a 1/12 scale Tudor dolls' house so that I could display some of the porcelain dolls that I'd dressed. I thoroughly enjoyed the research, designing and stitching the costumes as accurately as I could at such a small scale. I then decided to make some wall hangings for my Tudor house.

## The challenge of scale

The first problem I encountered working on miniature wall hangings was that, in true 1/12 scale, the stitches themselves would have to be very tiny. I knew that my eyesight wasn't really up to using silk gauze that had over a hundred stitches to the inch! I decided to compromise, and designed panels that had elements of the early designs scaled down to roughly 1/12 scale in overall size. Pleased with the designs, I started to build them into a small business, making them into kits that I could sell from home. This book includes some of the designs that I've created over the years.

## Creating miniature designs

This collection of designs is suitable for both miniature needlepoint enthusiasts and dolls' house collectors. I hope, too, that the collection will be useful for people who want to work the charted designs at different scales – for instance, collectors of 1/24 scale dolls' houses. In fact, this book was written partly in response to requests for my patterns in a form that can be adapted to different scales.

I received a tremendous amount of help from groups of dolls' house and miniatures collectors. Their comments were very valuable, and I'm extremely grateful to them. Many of the collectors I spoke to expressed a great interest in my designs, and talked about their own difficulties creating designs and stitching at a miniature scale on silk gauze. I can certainly sympathize here, as my eyesight has deteriorated considerably over the years, and I can now rarely manage the tiny stitches needed for the fine gauze. Creating my kits on 22-count and 24-count canvas solved some of these problems of scale.

## *Getting a balance*

When you want to stitch something at a miniature scale, whether you're basically a miniaturist or an embroiderer, certain problems crop up quite frequently. It's easy to be overwhelmed by the complexity of some pieces designed for dolls' houses, or to be put off by the miniature scale itself and the small stitches that are necessary. Or, with some complex designs, you can eventually be defeated by the sheer time needed to complete the project. As a result, I feel that it's important to make sure that the designs are reasonably simple, and not too small in scale nor too large in size. I hope that I've achieved this balance with the designs in the book.

The task I set myself in this book was to produce needlepoint miniatures that look quite fine when stitched, but which are not too difficult to sew, or too time-consuming. I also wanted the designs to be as authentic to each period as possible. The pieces are the sort of historical designs that would have been found in the houses, castles and religious institutions of each era, and the projects are fairly accurate representations of the historical artwork of the periods.

## *Picking and choosing*

Designing on a 24-count fabric seems to meet my criteria but, as I mentioned before, at this size the stitches are too big to create an

Six embroidered botanical panels dating from Tudor times; I've taken one of the panels as my inspiration for the Elizabethan Panel on page 100

exact 1/12 representation of an original piece. However, the overall finished size of each piece is certainly representative of the type of wall hanging that would have been found in its period.

Designing at this scale, I can often take only part of an original piece and adapt it to the design area. Complex Celtic designs, and faces from all eras, are particularly awkward to reproduce since there are really not enough stitches available to create very intricate patterns or shaded details. Canvases with double threads are sometimes used to overcome this problem with larger-scale stitching, but these canvases tend to have a low thread count and therefore aren't suitable for miniature work.

As a result, the pieces in this book aren't exact 1/12 scale replicas. What I have created is a series of projects in miniature, based on well-researched historical designs, which reflect the feel of the three eras: Celtic, medieval and Tudor. And, of course, the pieces aren't true tapestries, which are woven rather than stitched, and I make no excuse for this! The projects are worked on fabric and canvas, and will enable you to create individual items and themed collections that are suitable for a period dolls' house, or which can simply be used as miniature pictures for your home. The designs would also make wonderful greetings cards for special occasions.

## Choosing the project to stitch

The designs that I have used are mainly interpretations of Celtic, medieval and Tudor artwork or textile designs. Where possible, I've given approximate dates and the background for each design so that you can choose the best period piece for your dolls' house. I've simplified the designs and changed some colours so that the pieces are as uncomplicated as possible, although you will need a certain level of proficiency to complete some of the more complex designs.

I've tried to include projects that will be suitable for all levels of skill, and graded the designs accordingly. If you're new to stitching miniatures, why not start with one of the smaller projects, such as the Shield on page 52 or the Long Panel on page 104? This will build up your confidence to tackle some of the slightly more demanding designs.

Whichever designs you choose to stitch, I hope that you'll enjoy working them, and feel proud of your achievements. Most of all, I hope that you'll feel the urge to finish each piece you start, and perhaps gain the confidence to design and work your own miniature needlepoint.

## *Male and female*

When I was creating the designs for the wall hangings I felt that I should also take another factor into account: the small number of male collectors who had asked for designs that would appeal to them. This is where historical designs are very useful as a pattern source, as many were designed by male artists for the weavers and embroiderers of the time to use; wealthy households often employed artists to design tapestries for the ladies of the household to stitch.

Later, books of illustrations were also available; embroiderers then could adapt these for use on linen garments and other household items such as bedding, wall hangings, cushions and table carpets. The medieval period in particular saw males and females working side by side, embroidering in guild workshops, within noble households and in religious institutions.

Today, it seems that embroidery is predominantly a female craft, but I'd love to see the original balance of male and female designers and embroiderers restored. I suspect that the use of computer-aided designing may have some impact here; I've certainly noticed an increase in the number of male designers who are producing some fabulous work in all areas of needlecraft.

# *Changing scale*

A detail of the beautiful Steeple Aston Cope, dating from 1310-40, which I've used as inspiration for the Angel on Horseback on page 80

For each project you will find that, as well as the finished size of my stitched version, I've also given the measurements of the piece at various thread counts, so that the design can be worked in a range of different scales. This will help if you're a collector of 1/24 scale miniatures and want to work these designs on much finer canvas and silk gauze for your own collections – or if you want to scale the designs up to make into cushion covers etc. If you decide to work one of the pieces at a scale other than the ones mentioned, all you need is the stitch count and the canvas thread (or hole) count. Divide the number of stitches by the thread count of your canvas to find out the finished size of the worked piece.

# *Choosing colours*

On the key for each project you will find alternatives for each thread colour so that you can use either Anchor or DMC threads. At the back of the book, on page 117, you'll also find the closest Madeira equivalents for the colours used in the projects. On several of the projects, too, you will find charts or suggestions for working the design in different colourways. Don't feel that you have to follow my colour choices slavishly; try out other colourways to suit the decor of particular rooms.

# *Over to you*

I do hope that you enjoy this first collection of designs and that you'll make some wonderful heirloom pieces to give many years of pleasure to you, your family and friends. Also, don't forget that you are supposed to enjoy your embroidery, not find it a chore. Have some fun with it, experiment with the designs, change the colours, add some metallic threads, change the border designs – make the piece uniquely yours.

Be ambitious with the use of the designs. Wall hangings can be converted for use as other items in the dolls' house, such as bed hangings, carpets, table carpets and upholstery. At larger scales the designs can be used for cushions or rugs in the home. It doesn't matter if you make a mistake when you're working the design – I almost always add to the original design when I'm sewing, making improvements here and there, or changing a shade or two. Above all, I hope that you gain real pleasure from working these projects.

Linen cutwork cushion dating from Tudor times. The designs on this piece inspired the motifs on the Elizabethan Square on page 108

# Materials &
# equipment

## Threads

The threads that I've used in the photographed projects are stranded cottons from the DMC range, but on each key I've also given the conversion numbers for Anchor threads. (On page 117 you'll find the closest equivalents of the colours used in the Madeira range of stranded threads.)

With the exception of some metallic threads, I use two strands of stranded cotton thread throughout. On the 22-count and 24-count fabric, two strands of cotton give reasonable coverage of the fabric. Three strands would give even better coverage, but the overall effect seems much bulkier than with the two strands, and doesn't seem quite delicate enough if the finished piece is for a dolls' house.

## Fabrics and canvases

Fabric for needlework is said to have a *count*. For evenweave fabrics (those with evenly spaced horizontal and vertical threads) this is usually expressed as *tpi*; this describes the number of threads the fabric has per inch. The higher the thread count, the more holes/stitches to the inch. Canvases are sometimes described as having an *hpi*; this is the number of holes per inch. Again, the higher the hpi, the finer the fabric and the more stitches per inch.

I've experimented with various small-count canvases and have chosen to work the designs for this book on 24-count congress cloth; this is an evenweave fabric which is softer than the stiffer canvas. I find that it distorts less than canvas and is easier to block. Congress cloth is not always easy to find, though, so as a good alternative I suggest 22-count mono canvas, or petit point canvas.

If you do use congress cloth, be warned that there is a potential disadvantage too; it comes in quite a few different colours, some of which (I'm told) are not colourfast. So, be careful if you want to experiment with a coloured background cloth. It's also not an interlocked fabric and has a tendency to fray at the edges. Whatever fabric you use, try taping each edge with masking tape before you begin stitching; the tape prevents the edges of congress cloth from fraying, and also prevents your stitching threads becoming snagged by the ends of the background threads if you're using canvas.

The designs can also be worked on various other canvases and fabrics, but the thread count will determine the amount of stitching

The photograph shows a selection of the materials and equipment you'll need when stitching miniature needlepoint projects

thread and the size of the needle you'll need to work the project. 'Waste canvas' dissolves when it's wetted, and so isn't suitable for these projects. Interlock canvas is very useful if you can find it at the correct count; it doesn't fray, as the threads making up the canvas pass through, rather than under and over, each other. The disadvantage of interlock canvas is that it's more rigid than other canvases so is less suitable for projects which need some 'give' in them, such as chair-seat covers. However, finding interlock canvas in a small enough count for miniature work is difficult – which brings us back to silk gauze.

Swiss premium silk gauze is a costly product, but fortunately, if you want it for miniature stitchery, you'll only need to buy it in very small quantities. This very fine, interlocked mesh of silk threads is available in counts from 24 to over 100 holes per inch, and even in today's metric lifestyle, it's usually purchased by the square inch. The gauze is usually white, and its main use is for miniature projects such as dolls' house embroideries, embroideries for mounting in jewellery, and petit point.

To make it easier to work on, the gauze needs to be mounted in a frame before you begin stitching. The best kind of frame is one made from thick cardboard (e.g. mount board), with an aperture slightly smaller than the piece of gauze; the silk gauze is taped over the aperture to hold it in position. Some suppliers include a cardboard mount when you buy a piece of silk gauze.

If you want to use silk gauze for any of the projects in the book, the charts of alternative sizes will give you the final measurements for working on 34- or 60-count.

## Needles

Tapestry needles are used for needlepoint. Tapestry needles have round, or blunt, tips, so that they pass through the holes in the background fabric easily and smoothly without catching.

It's crucial to use the correct size of needle for the fabric or canvas you're working on, so that the piece doesn't become distorted; the needle should pass through the holes in the fabric without displacing any of the threads. I use a size 24 needle for the 22-count and 24-count fabrics. If you're working on fine linens you'll need a smaller needle: I use a size 26 needle on these (28- to 36-count), and on lower-count silk gauze. Beading needles, which are long and very fine, are often used with silk gauze and very fine fabrics.

I suggest that you have a number of needles available in your chosen size when you begin a project; it's useful to have some needles pre-threaded and ready for use rather than keep threading and unthreading one single needle.

# *Frames*

It's important to stitch the projects on a frame – especially if you're using canvas, which has a tendency to stretch and distort as it's worked. Tent stitch also has a slight distorting effect on the canvas. The shape of the fabric can be restored by 'blocking' it (see page 22) when the stitching is complete, but if you work the needlepoint on a frame this minimizes distortion and may eliminate the need for blocking altogether.

The larger designs in the book were worked on a 12in (30cm) frame with a roller bar, and I stitched the small projects on slot-together bar frames. The bar frames are simple to use, but you do need to take care to keep them square, otherwise the canvas will still distort. Edge your piece of fabric with masking tape, then simply pin it to the frame using drawing pins. Bar frames are readily available from needlework shops, or you can easily make one at home out of an old wooden picture frame. You can also buy bar frame packs that make up into a range of useful frame sizes: some packs are specially designed for miniature pieces. In addition I have a small table frame, which I find is very useful when I want to use both hands.

When you're working the designs the canvas should be wholly supported by the frame. Don't put any pressure on the work itself at any time, either by resting anything on top of the work, or by holding the canvas in your fingers instead of the frame.

Hoops are suitable for use on some of the finer fabrics, such as linens, but if you use a hoop make sure that you remove it from the work every time you finish a session of stitching, so that it doesn't stretch the fabric or leave a mark. Use a hoop that's large enough to surround the whole stitching area, so that you don't ever have to tighten it over stitched areas. To help protect the fabric, the hoop can be covered with a strip of fabric or bias binding tape – or position a piece of tissue paper between the fabric and the hoop, tearing away the section of tissue paper that lies over the stitching area. Don't use a hoop with canvas, as it will stretch and distort the canvas quite badly.

## Scissors

You'll need a pair of small, sharp-pointed embroidery scissors for cutting the threads without damaging the fabric; make sure they cut right up to the points, to avoid fraying the threads. You'll also need a larger pair of scissors to cut the fabric to the required size.

Keep your scissors only for cutting fabric and thread; don't use them for cutting paper or card, as this blunts them and makes them less efficient.

## Magnifying glasses

Because the pieces in this book are, by definition, quite small, you may feel that some extra magnification will make the work easier and help to prevent eye-strain. There are many different types of magnifying accessories available for needleworkers. The type you choose is a matter of personal preference, but also depends on how much you wish to spend, as some of the specialized magnifier/light combinations are very costly.

The simplest types of magnifying glasses are lenses mounted on a cord which you wear around your neck; these have a magnification factor of around two (so that everything appears twice as large as it really is). Other magnifiers are more sophisticated and more powerful; they are often incorporated into floor stands, and have some kind of light attachment.

Some of the magnifiers available have an extra-strength section built into the main lens; it looks rather like a bubble of raised glass. This small lens is more powerful than the main lens and is used to examine small areas of work in greater detail. It's also useful when it comes to threading your needle.

## *Your working environment*

Work in a well-lit and comfortable environment. A chair that will support your back while you work is a must, as is a good source of natural light for daytime working. I have a small, part-brick conservatory that I use as my studio. One corner has a large window on either side; I've positioned a comfortable, high-backed chair in that corner to gain maximum advantage from the daylight.

If you're choosing thread colours, this task is best done in daylight as the colours look different under artificial light. Although a good light source is necessary for your stitching, very bright daylight shining directly onto the fabric makes the colours look very washed out, making it almost as bad as artificial lighting for colour selection. A slightly shady spot surrounded by good light is my personal preference for sewing.

I use a magnifying glass on an adjustable and comfortable headband. When I need additional lighting, I use a small, adjustable halogen floor lamp, which also has a magnifying glass attachment and a clip to hold my pattern. 'Daylight' and halogen bulbs are very useful and readily available.

Just a further note on bright sunlight: do be careful not to leave, or display, your work (or your threads) in full sunlight, as you'll soon notice the intensity being bleached out of the colours. Framed pictures are also better away from direct sunlight for the same reason.

## *Laying tools*

Laying tools are optional accessories that I find particularly useful. They are blunt-ended implements, similar in shape to long, large tapestry needles, that are used when more than one strand of thread needs to be worked together.

Laying tools are available from needlework shops and suppliers, and come in various shapes and sizes. Some are made of metal, others of wood or plastic, and some are finer than others, according to the type of thread being used: a fine one is most suitable for these projects. The tool that I use fits comfortably on my finger, but others are held in the palm of the hand. Mine looks like a half-ring with a metal cocktail stick attached (see the illustration below).

Stitchers use laying tools in different ways to suit their own working practices. I place mine on the middle finger of my left hand: I bring the stitch up through the fabric and then, before I go back down through the fabric, I put the laying tool on top of the threads. My stitching thread is then worked over the projection (**a**) so that the thread can be straightened and untwisted before the tool is removed and the stitch completed (**b**). The threads lie much more neatly if you use a laying tool, and it really doesn't slow me down significantly. Unfortunately, I can only use this method when I have both hands free – that is, when my stitching is supported by a table frame or floor stand.

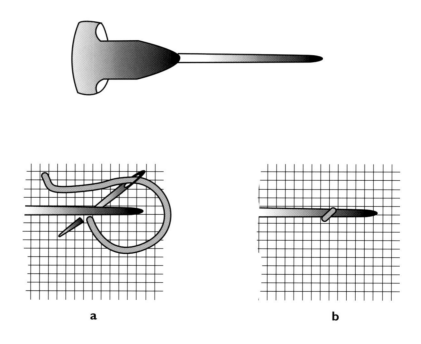

**a**                              **b**

# Stitching & finishing

## Selecting your materials

Before you begin to stitch a design, the first decision you need to make is: how will you be using the finished project? The answer to this question will determine how large you make the finished piece. The stated thread quantities with each design are for 22-count and 24-count fabric; you'll need to adjust the amount of thread and materials for any other size.

Once you've calculated the size of the finished design, you need to add a margin of fabric or canvas around all four sides of the stitching area. Allow at least 5cm (2in) all around if you intend to use the piece as a wall hanging, but allow at least 7.5cm (3in) on each side if the project is to be framed when it's completed.

For the larger projects, I allow at least enough canvas to ensure that I can mount the piece of fabric into a 12in frame. For the smaller pieces, don't use too small a frame; if the sewing area comes too close to the edges of the frame you'll have some difficulty stitching the outer areas.

Although fabric for stitching needlepoint is expensive, miniature projects – whatever their fabric count – only take a relatively small amount. When you've worked out the total size of fabric needed for your project, you can often buy exactly that amount, or a piece only slightly larger, from your usual needlecraft supplier.

## Preparing the fabric

It's useful to find the centre of your stitching area (particularly if you like to begin stitching in the centre of your designs). Do this by folding the fabric or canvas into four so that you can mark the centre

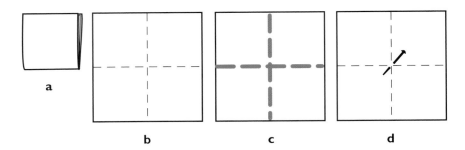

point (see **a** and **b** above). Some people like to stitch a contrasting guide thread down the centre lines (**c**) to help them count the squares and stitches, or you could mark them with a fading pen (marks made with a fading pen disappear within 24 hours), or simply insert a pin gently at the centre point (**d**). If you need to, you can mark the whole canvas out as a grid with the contrasting running thread or fading pen marking every tenth stitch. Personally I don't find this necessary, but if you're an inexperienced stitcher this approach may give you extra confidence.

Next, I cover each edge of the fabric or canvas with masking tape (as shown below). This helps prevent fraying of non-interlock canvas and also stops the threads from getting caught on the edges of the stiffer mono canvas. I then attach the canvas to a frame.

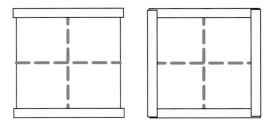

# Getting ready to stitch

Sort the threads (in daylight!) so that you are sure of the colours for each colour/symbol of the design. You may wish to keep several needles ready threaded, so that you don't have to keep stopping to re-thread the same needle.

Try not to use threads longer than about 40cm (16in); if you work with longer threads two things are likely to happen. First, the threads are more likely to twist and knot. Secondly: the thread always wears to some extent as you sew, because fibres are removed as you're constantly pulling it through the canvas, so the thread becomes thinner. You'll then find that it doesn't cover the canvas quite so efficiently. If you do see any thinning of the thread as you work, it's better to unpick the thinner stitches and start with a new thread in your needle, so that the texture of your stitching surface stays constant.

Position your chart where you can see it easily. (You may wish to use the black and white chart that can be photocopied and enlarged.) Some stitchers like to mark off their worked stitches with a highlighter pen as they sew; this reduces the risk of mistakes in counted-thread sewing, and you can still see the worked stitches through the colour of the highlighter if you need to rework an area.

# *The stitches*

The designs in this book are stitched using two different methods of producing a diagonal needlepoint stitch. The two methods of stitching look the same from the front of the work, but quite different from each other when you look at the back.

## Tent stitch

Tent stitch is used to sew the detailed areas of the designs. Tent stitch seems particularly appropriate for stitching these designs, as Tudor embroiderers frequently used it for their work. It's also sometimes known as 'Continental' stitch.

Come up through the fabric at the odd numbers and down where there is an even number indicated.

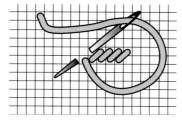 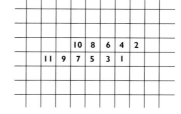

# Diagonal tent stitch

This is also known as 'basketweave' stitch as, on the reverse side, it resembles the interwoven lines of basketwork. It distorts the work slightly less than tent stitch, and is used for stitching larger areas of the designs and for filling in the background.

Follow the basic stitching sequence shown in the diagrams below, working across the canvas in diagonal rows. Again, bring the needle up through the canvas at the odd numbers and back down through it at the even numbers.

If you're a cross-stitcher, you'll have noticed that both stitches resemble the half cross-stitch that you're familiar with. Don't be tempted to use half cross-stitch instead of tent or diagonal tent stitch in these needlepoint designs: it doesn't cover the canvas so well, and it also has a much greater distorting effect on canvas.

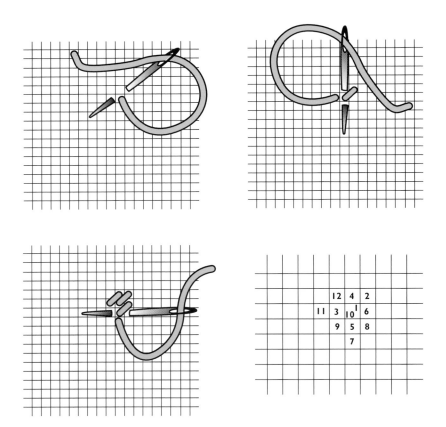

## Putting in a single stitch

There will be occasions on some designs where you need to work a single stitch in a particular colour. (Also, it's easy to miss a single stitch and not notice its omission until later!) In both these instances, follow these guidelines to drop the odd stitch into place with little effort.

Using a single strand of thread only, instead of the usual two, fold the thread in half and push the loop through the eye of your tapestry needle. Pull the thread so that the looped end is longer than the other end. Bring the thread up through the fabric and then down through the loop as you complete the stitch. The stitch is now fastened in place through the loop on the underside of your work and you will only have to sew in the remaining end of thread.

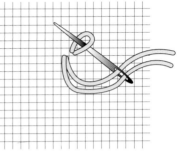

Wrong side of work

# Beginning the design

Once the canvas is on a frame, the sewing is generally worked in an up-and-down motion through the canvas, as shown in the diagrams below. This is sometimes referred to as a 'stabbing' action.

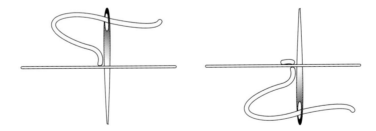

## Starting a thread

Put a knot in the end of the thread. Starting in the middle of the design area (unless instructed otherwise), pass the needle from the front of the work to the back about six stitches away from the position of the first stitch and in the direction in which you intend to sew. The knot is now on the front of the work. Bring the thread up

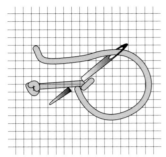

at the point you wish to make your first stitch, and sew towards the knot. When you reach the knot you can cut it off as close to your work as possible, taking great care not to cut into any of your worked stitches. The beginning of the thread is now securely anchored behind the worked stitches. Start any new threads in this way, making sure that each thread is properly anchored before cutting it off.

## Finishing a thread

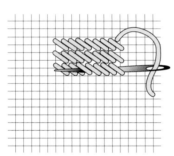

When you are coming to the end of a thread, pass the end through at least six stitches on the reverse of the work and then any remaining thread can be cut away. The thread is better anchored if it's finished horizontally or vertically – don't pass it diagonally through tent or basketweave stitches as it won't be held so securely. (This is probably because it's easy to miss some stitches as you thread through them diagonally.)

## Order of stitching

The order in which you build up a stitched design is really a matter of personal preference. Many people recommend that the detailed areas of any design are stitched first and then the background. Any areas in white are usually stitched last as this helps prevent the thread from becoming marked while working – it also helps prevent the white thread from picking up tiny fibres of other colours as they are worked.

The order of working a design really depends on the design itself. If a picture has a plain border, the central design is worked first and then the border – if you do it the other way round, it's easy to miscount the number of stitches in a plain border which may mean that the central design won't fit properly.

If the border has a regular geometric pattern, then this is usually worked first so that you can see that it works out correctly; any miscounting of stitches in geometric designs is very obvious. For the same reason it's best not to jump from area to area as you sew.

In some of the designs I recommend that the outlines of certain areas are worked first, and then filled in later. With each design I've given some guidance on a suggested stitching order, but as I've said it's far better to sew in your own style than to try and change your sewing practice significantly. There are no rights and wrongs, only suggestions that may help.

## *Following the charts*

Each design has both a colour and a black and white chart; you can work with whichever you prefer. On both types of chart, one square represents one stitch (the squares *do not* represent squares of the canvas). If you're working with a colour chart, the colour key alongside it indicates the colour you should use in your needle for each stitch on the chart.

The black and white charts use symbols in the squares; the key alongside the chart indicates the thread colour that should be used for each stitch marked with that symbol on the chart. This is particularly useful where several shades of one colour are used in a single design, or design area. The black and white charts will also help you if you prefer to enlarge and photocopy a chart and mark off the stitches as you work them.

All the keys show you the shades of DMC stranded cotton required, plus the Anchor equivalents (Madeira equivalents are on page 117). Alongside the numbers you'll find a colour description for each thread; these are only rough descriptions, not definitive names; they're to help you ensure that you're using the correct range of colours for the project. Don't be surprised if the same name, e.g. beige, is used for two slightly different colours in different projects.

Remember, too, that the colours available vary slightly from one manufacturer to another, so sometimes the equivalent given for a particular colour may be the closest match rather than an exact duplicate. This can be a significant disadvantage if you choose to use threads from a different manufacturer.

Sometimes, if there is no exact match for a particular colour in the new range, the manufacturer may give a near equivalent. This may result in the same shade being substituted for two (or more) colours in your original design. If this does happen, just choose a suitable alternative shade from the range available, or substitute your own colour choice.

# *Finishing*

When all the stitching is complete, remove the design from the frame. If the design is undistorted and the corners are still at true right-angles, then you can omit the blocking process described next. In practice, canvases are rarely truly square, anyway.

Cut away any excess canvas, leaving an unworked area around the design. If you're making the piece up into a wall hanging, leave enough canvas all around for a small hem; if the piece is to be framed, leave at least 7.5cm (3in) on each side.

## Blocking

If you have a blocking board, use drawing pins to secure the damp stitching to the board as shown below; use the lines on the board as guides to keep the work straight

Blocking is the technique used to restore a piece of needlework to its correct shape if it's been distorted during work. It's very easy to distort a piece of canvas. Canvas is stiffened with a component that softens when handled; as soon as this softening occurs, the piece readily stretches out of shape. (That's why using a frame while you're stitching minimizes distortion, as it reduces the handling of the fabric.) This stretching isn't necessarily distributed evenly across the canvas, so some areas may be more out of shape than others.

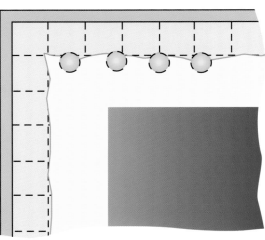

The blocking process uses a small amount of moisture to 're-size' the canvas. The damp canvas is pinned to a blocking board that is marked with straight lines; the edges of the fabric can be eased out straight and then pinned in position. You can easily make a blocking board at home; alternatively, use any piece of board into which you can put drawing pins (thumbtacks), and something with a right angle such as a set square or even an old picture frame.

To prepare the canvas for blocking, dampen it by steaming it thoroughly. Do be careful, as steam can produce a nasty scald. A steam iron can be used for this, or you can hold the fabric over boiling water (wearing rubber gloves to avoid the skin getting in contact with the steam). Don't let the fabric get too wet. The dressing on the canvas needs to be dampened, to loosen the weave, but if you make it too wet the dressing is simply flushed out of the canvas altogether.

You can use any rigid frame to block your stitching; the photograph shows a piece of work pinned to an old picture frame

Pin the canvas to your board, right side up, while it's still warm and damp, using the lines on the board or the corners of your right-angle to help you get the sides and corners of the finished work straight. (If you're using something wooden for your right angle, take care: wet wood may stain your work.)

Leave the canvas until it's completely dry, then you can remove it from the board for finishing.

If a canvas is very distorted, it can still be restored to its original shape. Use the blocking board and, after steaming the canvas, place it on top of a clean cloth with the worked design face down on the board. (Use a cloth which will not transfer colour to your design!) Pin the canvas to shape (face down), then gently rub thin wallpaper paste into the reverse of the design with your fingers, and leave the piece to dry for a few days. I've never needed to use this method myself when I've used a frame for working the designs, as the frame prevents the canvas from distorting too severely, but I'm told that it works a treat.

## Framing pictures

The designs look wonderful framed; look at the difference that the decorative frame has made to the Celtic Panel design (left), which

was also shown before framing on page 23. It's generally recommended that needlepoint isn't covered with glass, as it is a technique that's appreciated for its textures and feel as well as its looks, but the designs in this book are in regular, tiny needlepoint stitches and can be covered with glass if required. It certainly does help to prevent the work from attracting dust and dirt.

If you do need to get a needlepoint design cleaned, it's best to get it professionally dry-cleaned; I would never wash soiled needlepoint, as it destroys the dressing that holds the canvas in shape.

## Making up wall hangings

After blocking the work (if necessary), cut a piece of cotton or calico backing fabric to the same size as the canvas plus a little extra allowance all round for a small hem. Fold under the hem allowance on the canvas and press it carefully and lightly.

Choose a braid or matching ribbon that's suitable for making the hanging tabs. Decide how many tabs you would like your

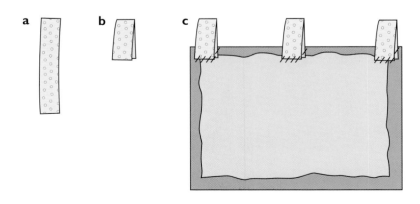

hanging to have, cut the ribbon or braid into the appropriate number of 6cm (2$^{1}/_{2}$in) lengths (**a**), and fold each tab in half (**b**). Fasten each tab with slip stitches to the reverse upper border of your canvas at even intervals (**c**).

Fold under a single hem all around the edge of the backing fabric, and press. The finished backing piece should be slightly smaller than the finished size of the wall hanging front. With wrong sides together, slip-stitch the backing piece to the reverse of the canvas, covering the places where the tabs are attached as you go (**d**).

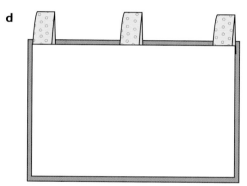

If you want to make the wall hanging lie flatter, you can use a layer of double-sided bonding web between the canvas and the backing fabric, or you can use a single-sided lightweight iron-on interfacing instead of the backing fabric. Be careful not to distort the canvas by over-ironing it.

## Making dolls' house carpets

Some of these designs could be adapted for use as carpets in later period dolls' houses. I haven't worked any of the designs as carpets, simply because carpets were so expensive to buy in Tudor times that mostly they were displayed on the walls or on tables – they were rarely walked on.

If you do want to make one of the stitched designs up as a floor carpet, omit the backing fabric and use a lightweight iron-on interfacing to cover the back of the canvas. This will cover the canvas hem and allow the carpet to lie flatter.

celtic designs

# celtic Inspirations

*t*HE CELTS (or Kelts), according to historical sources, originated in southern Germany, Bohemia and eastern France; from these regions they spread out to occupy vast land areas throughout Europe and parts of Asia Minor. In Britain, the Celts certainly occupied England, Wales and part of Scotland in the period we know as the Iron Age, about five hundred years before the birth of Christ.

## Learning about the Celts

We know little about the Celts from historical writing, as Celtic languages (the ancestors of Gaelic, Welsh and Breton) were spoken but not written down. Stories were handed down through the Celtic generations, but a lot of what we now believe to be true about the Celts is little more than educated guesswork. In fact, their enemies tell us more about the Celts than they do themselves. Some information can be gleaned from the few Latin writers who actually visited Britain during the period of Celtic occupation; one of these was Julius Caesar.

Most of our other information about the Celts has come from the study of Celtic artefacts and from excavation. By the year 613, the Celts had been virtually driven out of England by Anglo-Saxons following the Battle of Chester (during which the English were led by Aethelfrith of Northumbria). Fortunately, quite a lot of Celtic artwork has survived the centuries, particularly in metalwork and stone, and from this we can learn quite a lot about the Celtic way of life. We can also follow the path of artistic development in Britain quite clearly, as Christian and pagan art forms tend to be intertwined over the centuries.

## Celtic artwork

As time has passed we've discovered more and more about the Celtic way of life, and many artefacts have been found – from stone crosses (see frontispiece) to grave goods – which all bear testimony to the intricacy and sophistication of decorative Celtic art. Since the time they first appeared, Celtic designs have continued to be reproduced on such items as jewellery, clothing, decorative furnishings, weapons, manuscripts and needlework. Their popularity seems to have grown rather than diminished with time, and today you can

find them in almost every medium from wood to wool, as artists continue to draw on the fountain of Celtic art.

It's only when you're drawing or working the designs that you truly appreciate the skill that has gone into the creation of a Celtic piece. Geometric, often symmetrical, intricately interwoven patterns, interspersed with fantastic creatures, can only make us wonder at the inspiration which gave Celtic art its unrivalled character.

*Above:* Detail of a 'carpet page' design from the 7th-century Irish manuscript *The Book of Durrow*

## Using the designs in miniature

The sophistication of Celtic artwork probably isn't demonstrated at its best when you're working in miniature needlework with a limited number of stitches. It's exceedingly difficult truly to do justice to the wonderful designs without resorting to ever smaller stitch counts! Zoomorphic creatures do translate better than the intricate interlaced designs, and for this reason I've included two of them in this section, featuring some of the fantastical creatures that were used so many years ago. I've also included a knotwork design that has proved very popular (and I've suggested an alternative colour-way for it too). The Celtic Panel is a series of typical Celtic designs brought together with a slightly more modern theme.

# the celtic knot

*Celtic knots are perfect combinations of simplicity and complexity; this interwoven pattern is set into a diamond-shaped frame*

*t*HIS DESIGN HAS an abundance of potential uses. I've used it to decorate greetings cards, and as both a wall hanging and a bedhead for a dolls' house; it's even been stitched as a round coaster by adding extra stitches to the outside of the design. The design isn't bulky, and therefore will fit into many of the current needlework display products such as coasters, trinket-box lids, paperweights, etc.

As with all Celtic designs, this one has occurred in almost all the historical periods since the early days of the Celts. This is handy for the dolls' house or miniature collector concerned about authenticity, as the use of Celtic designs isn't limited to a specific era.

I love this design, but do be warned that it can lend itself to stitching errors. The placement of stitches is quite crucial if the knot pattern is to work out properly, and mistakes will be fairly obvious even though the piece is small.

## MATERIALS REQUIRED

- Cream congress cloth/24-count evenweave fabric approximately 13cm (5in) square minimum (or larger to fit your sewing frame)
- Frame, masking tape, drawing pins
- Fabric scissors and embroidery scissors

- Magnifying glass (optional)
- Tapestry needle(s) size 24
- Six-strand cotton thread:
  1 skein of each of:

|  | DMC | Anchor |
|---|---|---|
| Turquoise | 597 | 1064 |
| Dark cream | 677 | 361 |
| Green | 701 | 227 |
| Royal blue | 792 | 941 |

**STITCH COUNT:** 60 x 60

**FINISHED SIZE:**
6.4 x 6.4cm (2$\frac{1}{2}$ x 2$\frac{1}{2}$in)
on 24-count congress cloth

**ALTERNATIVE SCALES**
16-count: 9.5 x 9.5cm (3$\frac{3}{4}$ x 3$\frac{3}{4}$in)
22-count: 6.9 x 6.9cm (2$\frac{3}{4}$ x 2$\frac{3}{4}$in)
34-count: 4.5 x 4.5cm (1$\frac{3}{4}$ x 1$\frac{3}{4}$in)
60-count: 2.5 x 2.5cm (1 x 1in)

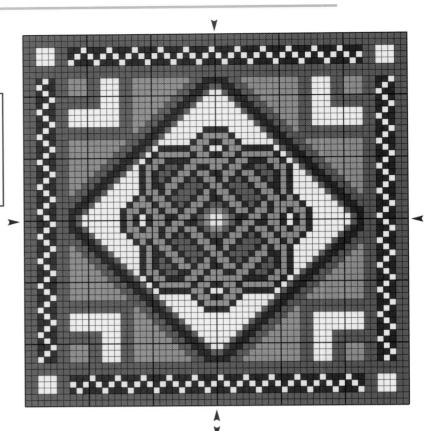

| **Key A** | DMC | Anchor |
|---|---|---|
| Turquoise | 597 | 1064 |
| Dark cream | 677 | 361 |
| Green | 701 | 227 |
| Royal blue | 792 | 941 |

Try this alternative colourway (**B**) for a rather different feel to the design. You will need one skein of each of the colours listed in the key below.

| **Key B** | DMC | Anchor |
|---|---|---|
| Sage green | 504 | 206 |
| Brown | 922 | 1003 |
| Dark grey | 924 | 851 |
| Sea green | 958 | 187 |

| Key A | DMC | Anchor |
|---|---|---|
| ⬭ Turquoise | 597 | 1064 |
| + Dark cream | 677 | 361 |
| − Green | 701 | 227 |
| ● Royal blue | 792 | 941 |

| Key B | DMC | Anchor |
|---|---|---|
| + Sage green | 504 | 206 |
| − Brown | 922 | 1003 |
| ● Dark grey | 924 | 851 |
| ⬭ Sea green | 958 | 187 |

### ∼ Stitching Tip ∼

Stitch the outer border of the design first, as it has a regular pattern. Once the border is complete, then stitch the central design. Or, if you prefer, stitch the entire design starting at the top right-hand corner and working diagonally across towards the bottom left.

# the celtic panel

*A Celtic cross forms the centrepiece of this rich design,
which can be readily adapted for a variety of projects*

*e*ARLY CELTIC STYLES of artwork were adapted by later artists, and spectacular examples can be seen in great works such as *The Book of Kells* and *The Lindisfarne Gospels.* The monastic artists in Ireland and Northumbria maintained a strong Celtic tradition in their craftsmanship, blending early Christian and pagan art forms. The Celtic crosses found around the British Isles are examples of this blend; they were erected on monastic sites, particularly in Ireland, from around the seventh and eighth centuries.

For the design of this panel, I've created a more modern interpretation of the Celtic theme. I've used a Celtic cross as the centrepiece of the design, and typical patterns of the time in the four outer sectors. This design makes a lovely gift card, but does require approximately 20 hours' work. It can also be used as a small wall hanging or even a carpet in the dolls' house, and makes a pretty framed picture. There are only four colours in this design, which makes it fairly inexpensive in materials.

### MATERIALS REQUIRED

- Cream congress cloth/24-count evenweave fabric approximately 15 x 18cm (6 x 7in) minimum (or larger to fit your sewing frame)
- Frame, masking tape, drawing pins
- Fabric scissors and embroidery scissors
- Magnifying glass (optional)
- Tapestry needle(s) size 24
- Six-strand cotton thread: 1 skein of each of:

|       | DMC | Anchor |
|-------|-----|--------|
| Red   | 606 | 334    |
| Green | 699 | 923    |
| Blue  | 796 | 133    |
| Flesh | 945 | 881    |

### STITCH COUNT: 71 x 91

### FINISHED SIZE:

7.5 x 9.6cm (3 x 3$^{3}$/4in) on 24-count congress cloth

### ALTERNATIVE SCALES

16-count: 11.3 x 14.4cm (4$^{1}$/2 x 5$^{5}$/8in)
22-count: 8.2 x 10.5cm (3$^{1}$/4 x 4$^{1}$/8in)
34-count: 5.3 x 6.8cm (2$^{1}$/8 x 2$^{3}$/4in)
60-count: 3 x 3.9cm (1$^{1}$/4 x 1$^{1}$/2in)

## ∼ *Stitching Tip* ∼

This is a really easy design to stitch. It has a regular border pattern, so stitch this first. Then, start in the middle with the cross and work the red outlines to the rectangles before filling in the middle of each. Stitch counting is easy with this design. Experiment with alternative colour schemes; you need four colours that are a good contrast to each other.

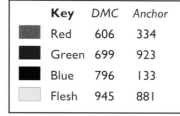

| Key | DMC | Anchor |
|---|---|---|
| Red | 606 | 334 |
| Green | 699 | 923 |
| Blue | 796 | 133 |
| Flesh | 945 | 881 |

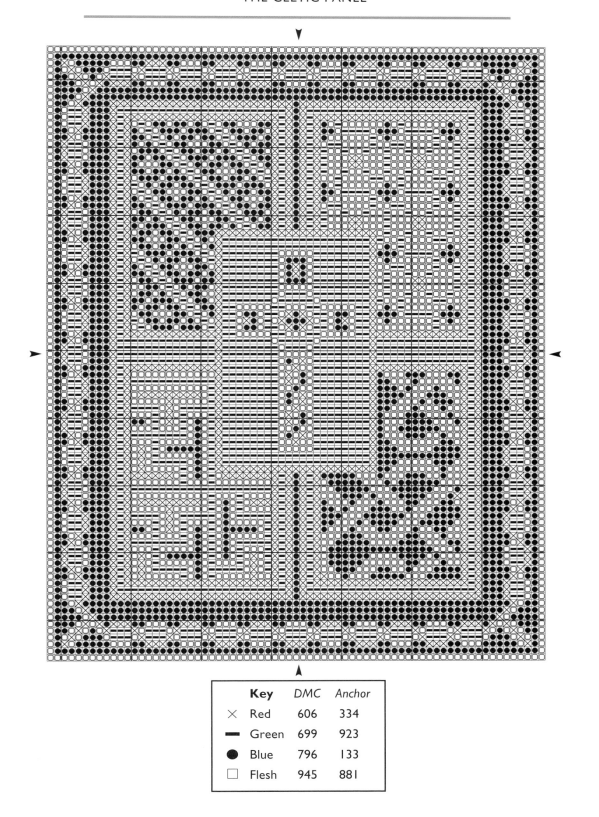

| Key | DMC | Anchor |
|---|---|---|
| × Red | 606 | 334 |
| — Green | 699 | 923 |
| ● Blue | 796 | 133 |
| □ Flesh | 945 | 881 |

# zoomorphic panel

*The exaggerated neck, beak and claw of this bird are typical of the Celtic approach to our feathered friends!*

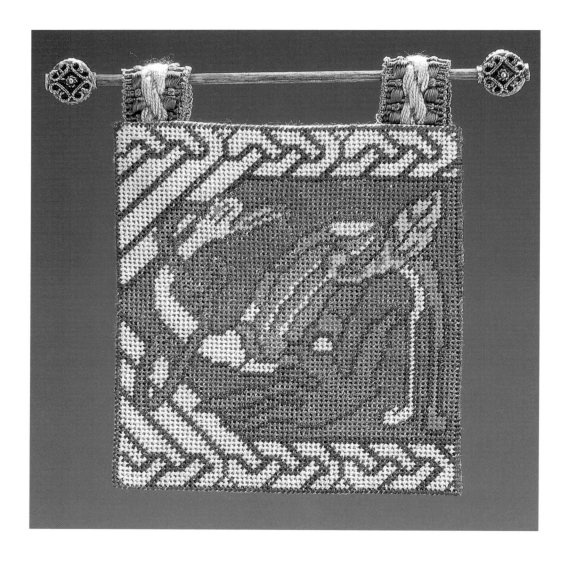

ZOOMORPH IS THE TECHNICAL TERM used for the Celtic interpretation of an animal or other living creature in a design; these zoomorphic depictions are almost always fantastical in design, although still recognizable as animals. As well as birds, such as the one shown here, creatures depicted include lions, fish, hounds, wolves, snakes and also human figures. Some of the animals have symbolic significance but others are purely for decoration.

The heads of the creatures are usually quite detailed and the bodies are elongated so that their limbs become part of elaborate knotwork designs. Many of the fiercer creatures appear to be devouring each other, as the legs of one animal come perilously close to the mouth of another. Zoomorphic forms are also found incorporated into the beautiful lettering typical of *The Book of Kells*, *The Lindisfarne Gospels* and *The Book of Durrow*. Zoomorphs are particularly used as part of the border art on the so-called 'carpet' pages of the books (designs which cover entire pages with a carefully arranged pattern).

The design on this panel is a typical Celtic depiction of a bird; it's a very simplified shape, which makes it very easy to stitch, and it's equally easy to experiment with other colourways. Allow about 10 hours to stitch this design.

## MATERIALS REQUIRED

- Cream congress cloth/24-count evenweave fabric approximately 15 x 18cm (6 x 7in) minimum (or larger to fit your sewing frame)
- Frame, masking tape, drawing pins
- Fabric scissors and embroidery scissors
- Magnifying glass (optional)
- Tapestry needle(s) size 24

- Six-strand cotton thread: I skein of each of:

|  | DMC | Anchor |
|---|---|---|
| Pale blue | 341 | 117 |
| Light tan | 436 | 363 |
| Pale green | 503 | 876 |
| Turquoise | 518 | 1039 |
| Burgundy | 815 | 44 |
| Mushroom | 842 | 1080 |
| Dark slate | 930 | 1035 |
| Orange | 971 | 316 |
| Yellow | 3820 | 306 |

**STITCH COUNT:** 72 x 80

**FINISHED SIZE:**
7.6 x 8.5cm (3 x 3³/8in)
on 24-count congress cloth

## ALTERNATIVE SCALES
16-count: 11.4 x 12.7cm (4¹/2 x 5in)
22-count: 8.3 x 9.2cm (3¹/4 x 3⁵/8in)
34-count: 5.4 x 6cm (2¹/8 x 2³/8in)
60-count: 3 x 3.4cm (1¹/4 x 1³/8in)

| **Key A** | DMC | Anchor |
|---|---|---|
| Pale blue | 341 | 117 |
| Light tan | 436 | 363 |
| Pale green | 503 | 876 |
| Turquoise | 518 | 1039 |
| Burgundy | 815 | 44 |
| Mushroom | 842 | 1080 |
| Dark slate | 930 | 1035 |
| Orange | 971 | 316 |
| Yellow | 3820 | 306 |

### ∾ *Stitching Tip* ∾

This is one of the easiest designs to sew. Begin with the knotwork border design at the top right-hand corner. Work the border across the top, then start at the bottom left-hand corner of the design and work the border across the bottom of the design. The outline of the bird comes next: then fill in the details. Finally fill in the background colour.

| Key B | DMC | Anchor |
|---|---|---|
| Rust | 436 | 363 |
| Turquoise | 518 | 1039 |
| Sage green | 522 | 860 |
| Dark red | 600 | 59 |
| Mushroom | 842 | 1080 |
| Dark slate | 930 | 1035 |
| Light green | 966 | 240 |
| Tangerine | 972 | 298 |
| Beige | 3047 | 852 |

The alternative colour scheme (**B**) shown here produces a totally different effect. For this version, you'll need one skein of each of the colours mentioned in the key.

| **Key A** | DMC | Anchor |
|---|---|---|
| ☐ Pale blue | 341 | 117 |
| ✕ Light tan | 436 | 363 |
| ∧ Pale green | 503 | 876 |
| ⊺ Turquoise | 518 | 1039 |
| ⬉ Burgundy | 815 | 44 |
| ♡ Mushroom | 842 | 1080 |
| ▶ Dark slate | 930 | 1035 |
| ◀ Orange | 971 | 316 |
| + Yellow | 3820 | 306 |

| **Key B** | DMC | Anchor |
|---|---|---|
| ✕ Rust | 436 | 363 |
| ∧ Turquoise | 518 | 1039 |
| ☐ Sage green | 522 | 860 |
| ◀ Dark red | 600 | 59 |
| ♡ Mushroom | 842 | 1080 |
| ▶ Dark slate | 930 | 1035 |
| ⊺ Light green | 966 | 240 |
| + Tangerine | 972 | 298 |
| ⬉ Beige | 3047 | 852 |

# celtic birds

*These two birds, in dramatic plumage, seem to be
having a romantic tryst*

I THINK THIS DESIGN is rather romantic: it reminds me of love-birds. Two birds so intimately locked together are rather unusual in Celtic design; more usually, the Celtic zoomorphs are either chasing each other or fighting. These are obviously much more pleasant creatures, completely lacking in aggression!

I chose this second bird motif for its simplicity; it's an easy-to-sew design, and is perfect for beginners to needlepoint. You'll need roughly 10 hours to complete the stitching.

The background may seem a little daunting, as it's all filled in with one colour; if you don't like the idea of this much background stitching, try sewing the bird design on a coloured, evenweave fabric (use an aida fabric if you are a beginner), using cross-stitch instead of needlepoint. Omit the background stitches and leave the coloured evenweave fabric showing, and it will be much quicker to stitch while still giving you a nicely textured design.

### MATERIALS REQUIRED

- Cream congress cloth/24-count evenweave fabric approximately 15 x 18cm (6 x 7in) minimum (or larger to fit your sewing frame)
- Frame, masking tape, drawing pins
- Fabric scissors and embroidery scissors
- Magnifying glass (optional)
- Tapestry needle(s) size 24

- Six-strand cotton thread: 1 skein of each of:

|  | DMC | Anchor |
|---|---|---|
| Turquoise | 518 | 1039 |
| Beige | 712 | 926 |
| Pale yellow | 744 | 301 |
| Light salmon | 945 | 881 |
| Dark rose | 3722 | 1027 |
| Dark green | 3808 | 1068 |
| Light green | 3813 | 875 |

### STITCH COUNT: 103 x 80

### FINISHED SIZE:

10.9 x 8.5cm (4$^{1}$/4 x 3$^{1}$/4in) on 24-count congress cloth

### ALTERNATIVE SCALES

16-count: 16.4 x 12.7cm (6$^{1}$/2 x 5in)
22-count: 11.9 x 9.2cm (4$^{3}$/4 x 3$^{5}$/8in)
34-count: 7.7 x 6 cm (3 x 2$^{3}$/8in)
60-count: 4.4cm x 3.4cm (1$^{3}$/4 x 1$^{3}$/8in)

### ∾ *Stitching Tip* ∾

Begin by sewing the plain border. Start in the centre
and work the outline of the birds, then the two panels
at the top and bottom of the design. Finally, fill in the
design and then stitch in the background colour.

| **Key A** | DMC | Anchor |
|---|---|---|
| Turquoise | 518 | 1039 |
| Beige | 712 | 926 |
| Pale yellow | 744 | 301 |
| Light salmon | 945 | 881 |
| Dark rose | 3722 | 1027 |
| Dark green | 3808 | 1068 |
| Light green | 3813 | 875 |

| **Key B** | DMC | Anchor |
|---|---|---|
| Yellow-green | 471 | 265 |
| Orange | 744 | 301 |
| Light blue | 747 | 158 |
| Tan | 782 | 308 |
| Turquoise | 807 | 168 |
| Dark green | 3808 | 1068 |
| Dark straw | 3820 | 306 |

Try a more vibrant version of the birds using the colourway (**B**) shown here. For this version, you'll need one skein of each of the colours in the key.

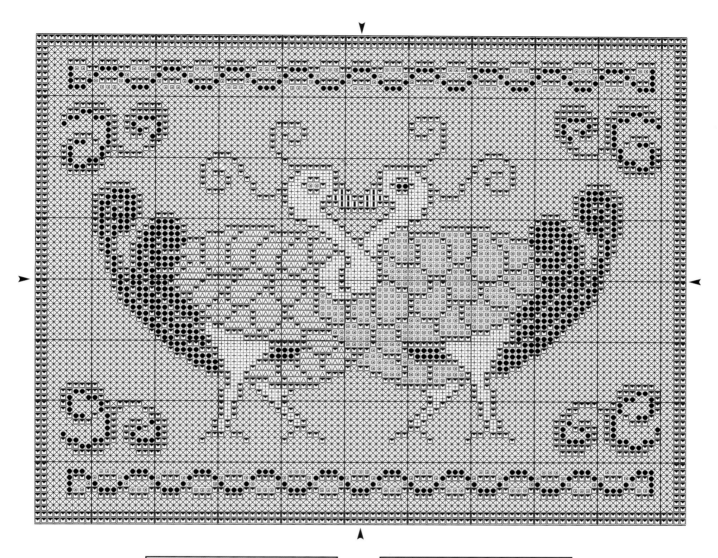

| | **Key A** | DMC | Anchor |
|---|---|---|---|
| △ | Turquoise | 518 | 1039 |
| + | Beige | 712 | 926 |
| ❙ | Pale yellow | 744 | 301 |
| ✕ | Light salmon | 945 | 881 |
| ⊡ | Dark rose | 3722 | 1027 |
| ☷ | Dark green | 3808 | 1068 |
| ● | Light green | 3813 | 875 |

| | **Key B** | DMC | Anchor |
|---|---|---|---|
| △ | Yellow-green | 471 | 265 |
| ⊡ | Orange | 744 | 301 |
| + | Light blue | 747 | 158 |
| ❙ | Tan | 782 | 308 |
| ● | Turquoise | 807 | 168 |
| ☷ | Dark green | 3808 | 1068 |
| ✕ | Dark straw | 3820 | 306 |

# Medieval Designs

# 𝕸𝖊𝖉𝖎𝖊𝖛𝖆𝖑 𝕴𝖓𝖘𝖕𝖎𝖗𝖆𝖙𝖎𝖔𝖓𝖘

I T WAS WHILE I was searching through a wealth of medieval art and textile designs that I first realized the enormous potential for making small wall hangings for dolls' houses. The designs were just crying out to be miniaturized, with their strong, simple shapes and glorious colours.

I don't in any way mean to insult this subtle, complex art form by describing medieval art and design as 'simple.' The designs may lack the perspective that we're familiar with from later historical periods, and perhaps some of the detail and shading that occur in more recent art, but medieval art has a unique, compulsive quality all of its own.

## Uses of medieval art

This popular medieval depiction of an imbibing monk inspired my Cellarer panel on page 68

Art was frequently used by the churches and religious institutions of the day to put across moral messages, and some of these messages were intended to be truly terrifying. Images of death and the sinner were very frequent, as were other images of illness and death, such as victims of plague, skeletons, mourning figures and surgery. Seeing these images today reminds us of the precarious nature of life in medieval times. Not all the images were so gruesome, though, as other pieces of art and embroidery showed rural scenes of farming, hunting and wildlife, along with images of everyday life such as childbirth, cooking, life at court, love, sports and pastimes.

## The stitchers

The churches were quite wealthy at this time and could afford to employ some of the most skilled craftsmen and women to produce wonderful works in silk, silver and silver-gilt threads. Unfortunately, because so many of these professional embroiderers were operating from family workshops, there is little or no documentary evidence of their identity, although some workshops did use well-known artists to draw up their designs for them. It's through their efforts that we have such a glorious legacy that weaves the story of life in medieval Europe.

Wall hangings were very popular in the wealthy households of the time, and necessary items in an era of draughty castles and manor houses. English wall hangings were usually made by embroiderers rather than weavers; the Bayeaux Tapestry, for example, is not a true tapestry as it's created in surface embroidery applied to a ready-woven background.

Woven tapestries were usually much warmer and thicker than the embroidered wall hangings, but often had to be imported from other countries and were excessively costly.

## Woven or stitched?

Today, we also often apply the word 'tapestry' to our own canvaswork or needlepoint (the application of various embroidery stitches to a ready-woven background fabric). We can buy 'tapestry' canvas which is sometimes printed with a design, or we can put our own counted threadwork designs onto it. There is a distinction, though, between this type of work and true tapestries. True tapestries are actually woven pictures, worked on looms in highly specialized workshops; the coloured threads that form the picture are actually part of the woven fabric itself rather than something stitched onto it afterwards. (With this in mind I chose to call the designs in this book wall hangings rather than tapestries.)

There was no difficulty at all finding designs and motifs for this period, rather a problem of which designs to leave out. Consequently, this section is a little larger than the other two sections in this book – I'm afraid I just got carried away!

# The Shield

*Every respectable ancient dolls' house and castle needs its own coat of arms; this adaptable pattern ensures that you can design one to suit your miniature knights*

$\mathfrak{I}$ DESIGNED THIS SIMPLE PANEL in response to requests from owners of dolls' castles who wanted a small shield that was easy to stitch. You can't get much easier than this design! Although I did refer to relevant books, I can't claim any great knowledge of the rules of heraldry, so I do apologize for any anachronisms in the design.

This is an easy design, and an ideal starter if you haven't done any needlepoint before. The stitching took me about four hours to complete; add a bit longer if you're a beginner. One of my daughters tackled this design when she was 13 years old; she was a complete beginner to needlepoint, but didn't have any problems.

This design has a large range of uses. Try fitting the shield into a frame or a greetings card, or make yourself a set of coasters. You could even add your own motifs to the basic shape.

## MATERIALS REQUIRED

- Cream congress cloth/24-count evenweave fabric approximately 10cm (4in) square minimum (or larger to fit your sewing frame)
- Frame, masking tape, drawing pins
- Fabric scissors and embroidery scissors
- Magnifying glass (optional)
- Tapestry needle(s) size 24

- Six-strand cotton thread:
  1 skein of each of:

| | DMC | Anchor |
|---|---|---|
| Light brown | 642 | 392 |
| Green | 700 | 228 |
| Grey | 762 | 234 |
| Blue | 797 | 132 |
| Red | 817 | 13 |
| Dark brown | 838 | 1088 |
| Mid brown | 840 | 1084 |

**STITCH COUNT:** 50 x 49

**FINISHED SIZE:**
5.3 x 5.2cm (2$^{1}$/8 x 2in)
on 24-count congress cloth

**ALTERNATIVE SCALES**
16-count: 7.9 x 7.8cm (3$^{1}$/8 x 3$^{1}$/8in)
22-count: 5.8 x 5.7cm (2$^{1}$/4 x 2$^{1}$/4in)
34-count: 3.7 x 3.7cm (1$^{1}$/2 x 1$^{1}$/2in)
60-count: 2.1 x 2.1cm ($^{7}$/8 x $^{7}$/8in)

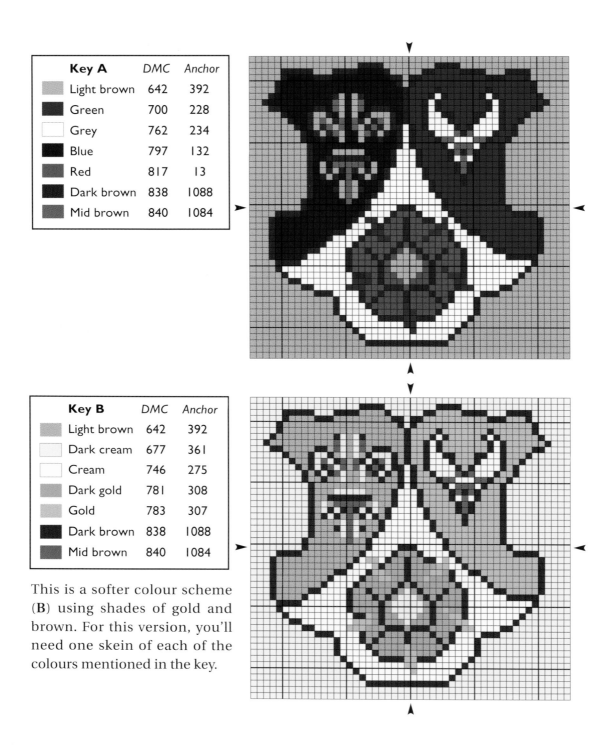

| **Key A** | DMC | Anchor |
|---|---|---|
| Light brown | 642 | 392 |
| Green | 700 | 228 |
| Grey | 762 | 234 |
| Blue | 797 | 132 |
| Red | 817 | 13 |
| Dark brown | 838 | 1088 |
| Mid brown | 840 | 1084 |

| **Key B** | DMC | Anchor |
|---|---|---|
| Light brown | 642 | 392 |
| Dark cream | 677 | 361 |
| Cream | 746 | 275 |
| Dark gold | 781 | 308 |
| Gold | 783 | 307 |
| Dark brown | 838 | 1088 |
| Mid brown | 840 | 1084 |

This is a softer colour scheme (**B**) using shades of gold and brown. For this version, you'll need one skein of each of the colours mentioned in the key.

| **Key A** | | DMC | Anchor |
|---|---|---|---|
| ☐ | Light brown | 642 | 392 |
| ● | Green | 700 | 228 |
| ▽ | Grey | 762 | 234 |
| ■ | Blue | 797 | 132 |
| ▶ | Red | 817 | 13 |
| ▼ | Dark brown | 838 | 1088 |
| — | Mid brown | 840 | 1084 |

| **Key B** | | DMC | Anchor |
|---|---|---|---|
| ■ | Light brown | 642 | 392 |
| ☐ | Dark cream | 677 | 361 |
| ▽ | Cream | 746 | 275 |
| ▶ | Dark gold | 781 | 308 |
| ● | Gold | 783 | 307 |
| ▼ | Dark brown | 838 | 1088 |
| — | Mid brown | 840 | 1084 |

## ∼ *Stitching Tips* ∼

I suggest that you tackle the shield outline first, then divide the interior of the shield into its three design areas and work the detail of each one at a time. Finally, complete the background colours of the shield and then the background of the outer area.

Also, don't be put off by the slightly asymmetrical look of the design when you've stitched the outline of the shield. In needlepoint all the stitches should slope the same way. This always makes diagonal border lines look strange, as the right-sloping diagonal appears as a straight line while the left appears as a broken line of small stitches.

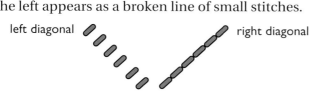

left diagonal          right diagonal

# The Tournament

*The colour and vibrancy of medieval pageantry are
brought to life in this dramatic panel*

TWO JOUSTING KNIGHTS at a tournament are depicted in this project, taken from a manuscript dated around 1445. The manuscript was actually a series of illustrations showing the coats of arms of individual knights of the time. Medieval armour was rarely particularly distinctive, so knights took to displaying their coats of arms on their shields as a means of identification in battle. Later the same design would be used on the knight's robe, banner, his horse's caparison and sometimes even on his wife's outfit as well.

I particularly like the simplicity of this design. There are fairly large blocks of colour that make the project easy to sew even though it's quite large – for a 1/12 scale miniature. Don't be put off by this, though, as wall hangings and tapestries were intended to cover large expanses of wall.

## MATERIALS REQUIRED

- Cream congress cloth/24-count evenweave fabric, 30cm (12in) square minimum, or an appropriate size to fit on the roller frame
- 12in roller frame
- Fabric scissors and embroidery scissors
- Magnifying glass (optional)
- Tapestry needle(s) size 24
- Six-strand cotton thread: 3 skeins of:

| | DMC | Anchor |
|---|---|---|
| Mushroom | 644 | 391 |
| 1 skein of each of: | | |
| Deep red | 321 | 47 |
| Chestnut | 434 | 310 |
| Dark grey | 645 | 273 |
| Mid grey | 647 | 1040 |
| Light grey | 648 | 900 |
| Gold | 783 | 307 |
| Navy blue | 791 | 178 |
| Mid blue | 825 | 162 |
| Dark brown | 838 | 1088 |
| Mid brown | 840 | 1084 |
| Orange | 921 | 1003 |

**STITCH COUNT:** 200 x 135

**FINISHED SIZE:**
21.2 x 14.3cm ($8^{1}/2$ x $5^{5}/8$in)
on 24-count congress cloth

**ALTERNATIVE SCALES**
16-count: 31.8 x 21.4cm ($12^{1}/2$ x $8^{1}/2$in)
22-count: 23.1 x 15.6cm ($9^{1}/8$ x $6^{1}/8$in)
34-count: 14.9 x 10.1cm ($5^{7}/8$ x 4in)
60-count: 8.5 x 5.7cm ($3^{3}/8$ x $2^{1}/4$in)

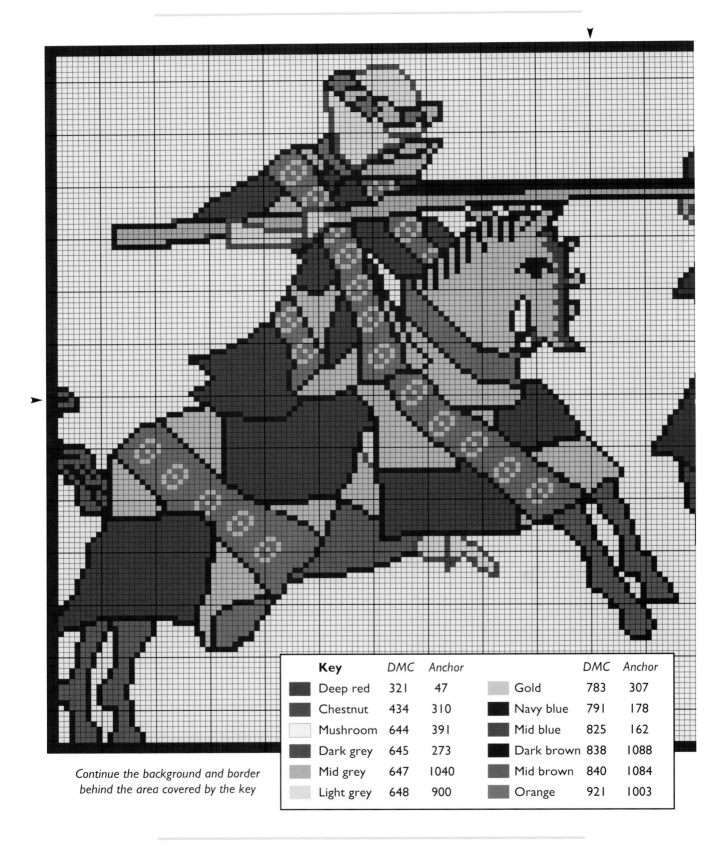

*Continue the background and border
behind the area covered by the key*

| **Key** | DMC | Anchor | | DMC | Anchor |
|---|---|---|---|---|---|
| Deep red | 321 | 47 | Gold | 783 | 307 |
| Chestnut | 434 | 310 | Navy blue | 791 | 178 |
| Mushroom | 644 | 391 | Mid blue | 825 | 162 |
| Dark grey | 645 | 273 | Dark brown | 838 | 1088 |
| Mid grey | 647 | 1040 | Mid brown | 840 | 1084 |
| Light grey | 648 | 900 | Orange | 921 | 1003 |

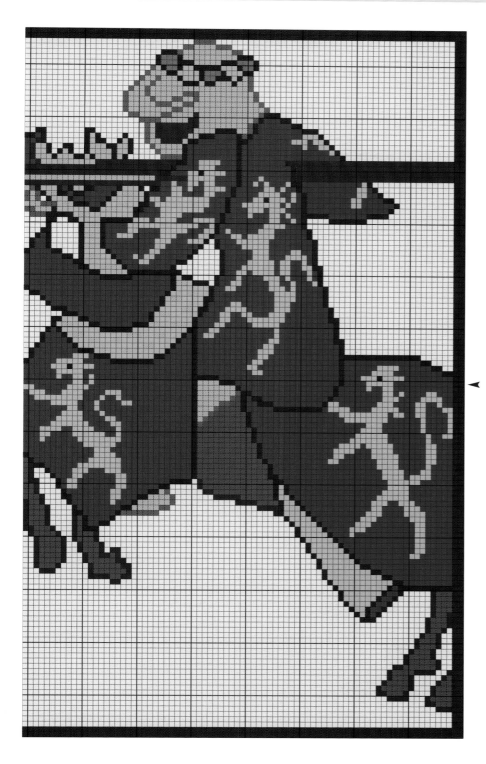

### ∾ *Stitching Tip* ∾

This design is far easier to stitch than it looks. Start in the centre of the design and work the outlines of the knights and horses, then fill in the details. Stitch the coloured areas on the coats of arms and the armour; finally, stitch the border and then fill in the background. If you prefer, these designs can be stitched in cross stitch on a coloured aida (to match the background colour); then the stitching behind the motifs can be omitted.

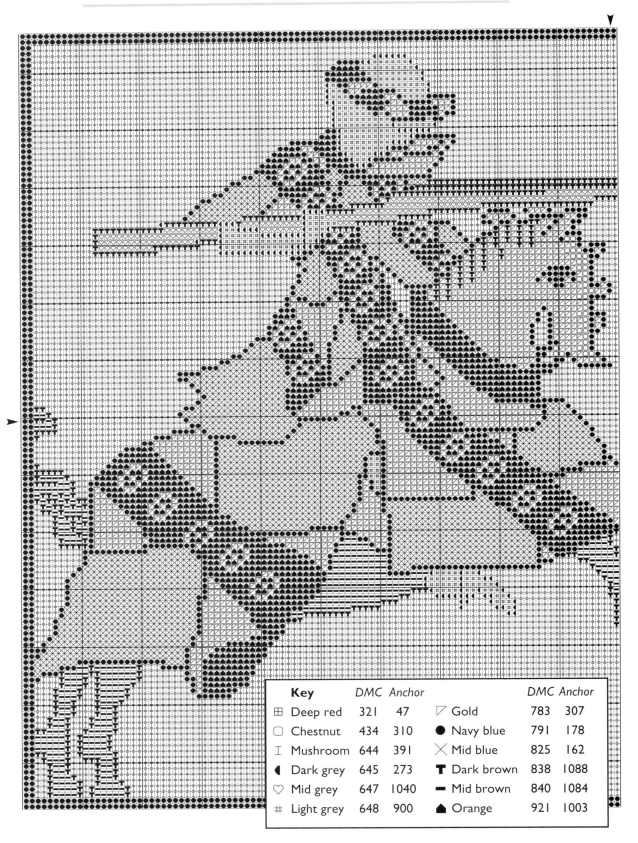

| **Key** | DMC | Anchor | | DMC | Anchor |
|---|---|---|---|---|---|
| ⊞ Deep red | 321 | 47 | ▽ Gold | 783 | 307 |
| ☐ Chestnut | 434 | 310 | ● Navy blue | 791 | 178 |
| I Mushroom | 644 | 391 | ✕ Mid blue | 825 | 162 |
| ◀ Dark grey | 645 | 273 | T Dark brown | 838 | 1088 |
| ♡ Mid grey | 647 | 1040 | — Mid brown | 840 | 1084 |
| # Light grey | 648 | 900 | ▲ Orange | 921 | 1003 |

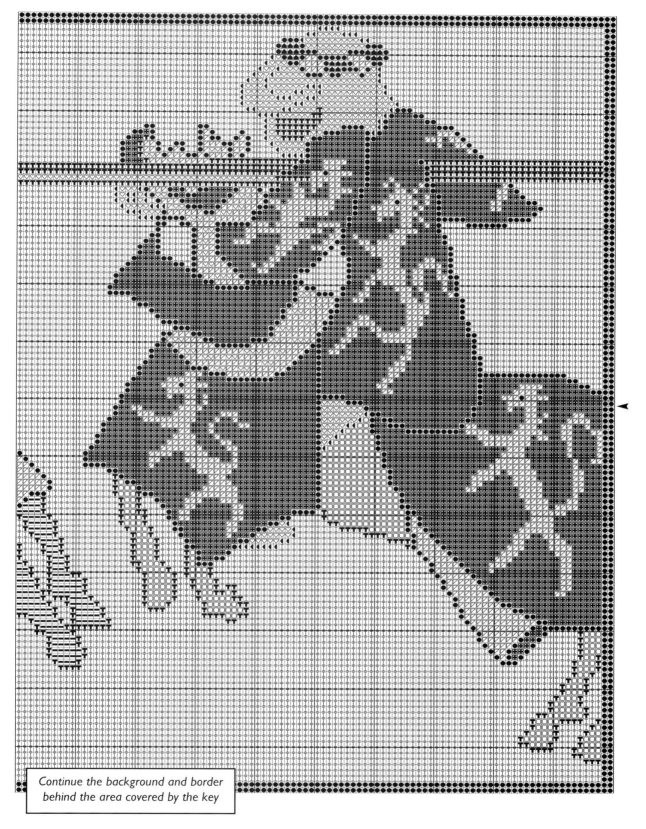

Continue the background and border
behind the area covered by the key

# Medieval Minstrels

*Imagine yourself at a medieval banquet with the sound of lute, rebec and recorder drifting down from the minstrels' gallery*

ON THIS HANGING, minstrels are shown playing a lute and a rebec (an instrument of the time that's an ancestor of the violin family). The design is adapted from an illumination of two Spanish minstrels from the *Cántigas de Santa Maria*, an anthology of Marian hymns compiled in the late thirteenth century. My interpretation, shown in the photograph, is much brighter than the original, but if you prefer colours that are more muted, and therefore closer to the original, try working the background lattice in a golden orange on a dark brown ground, with the main border stitched in a dark blue-green. You could then use a dark plum and the golden orange for the patterned border down the right-hand side.

This design is intentionally large, and would suit a large, dramatic room in a grand dolls' house or a castle. If the rooms in your dolls' house are smaller you may prefer to work the design in a finer count for a 1/12 scale dwelling. The stitching takes at least 40 hours to complete, so allow several weeks for working this project.

## MATERIALS REQUIRED

- Cream congress cloth/24-count evenweave fabric, 30cm (12in) square minimum, or an appropriate size to fit on the roller frame
- 12in roller frame
- Fabric scissors and embroidery scissors
- Magnifying glass (optional)
- Tapestry needle(s) size 24
- Six-strand cotton thread:

2 skeins of:

| | DMC | Anchor |
|---|---|---|
| Pale blue | 828 | 9159 |

1 skein of each of:

| | | |
|---|---|---|
| Deep rose | 223 | 895 |
| Purple | 333 | 119 |
| Mid brown | 434 | 310 |
| Grey-brown | 642 | 392 |
| Silver | 928 | 274 |
| Grey-blue | 931 | 1034 |
| Dark brown | 3371 | 382 |
| Flesh | 3774 | 778 |

## STITCH COUNT: 191 x 147

## FINISHED SIZE:

20.2 x 15.7cm (8 x 6¼in) on 24-count congress cloth

## ALTERNATIVE SIZES

16-count: 30.3 x 23.5cm (12 x 9¼in)
22-count: 22.1 x 17.1cm (8¾ x 6¾in)
34-count: 14.3 x 11.1cm (5⅝ x 4⅜in)
60-count: 8.1 x 6.3cm (3⅛ x 2½in)

## ∿ *Stitching Tip* ∿

Although it takes quite a while to stitch, the design itself is not particularly difficult. The background pattern probably takes longer to stitch than the minstrels themselves because you need to make sure that you get this pattern correct. I started with the criss-cross of the tiling, then stitched the outlines of the minstrels; I then completed the detail of the minstrels and their costumes before stitching the background of the main panel. This is one occasion where it pays to leave the outer border until last.

| Key | DMC | Anchor |
|---|---|---|
| Deep rose | 223 | 895 |
| Purple | 333 | 119 |
| Mid brown | 434 | 310 |
| Grey-brown | 642 | 392 |
| Pale blue | 828 | 9159 |
| Silver | 928 | 274 |
| Grey-blue | 931 | 1034 |
| Dark brown | 3371 | 382 |
| Flesh | 3774 | 778 |

| **Key** | DMC | Anchor |
|---|---|---|
| ☐ Deep rose | 223 | 895 |
| ► Purple | 333 | 119 |
| ▬ Mid brown | 434 | 310 |
| ✕ Grey-brown | 642 | 392 |
| △ Pale blue | 828 | 9159 |
| ♡ Silver | 928 | 274 |
| + Grey-blue | 931 | 1034 |
| ⬟ Dark brown | 3371 | 382 |
| ∣ Flesh | 3774 | 778 |

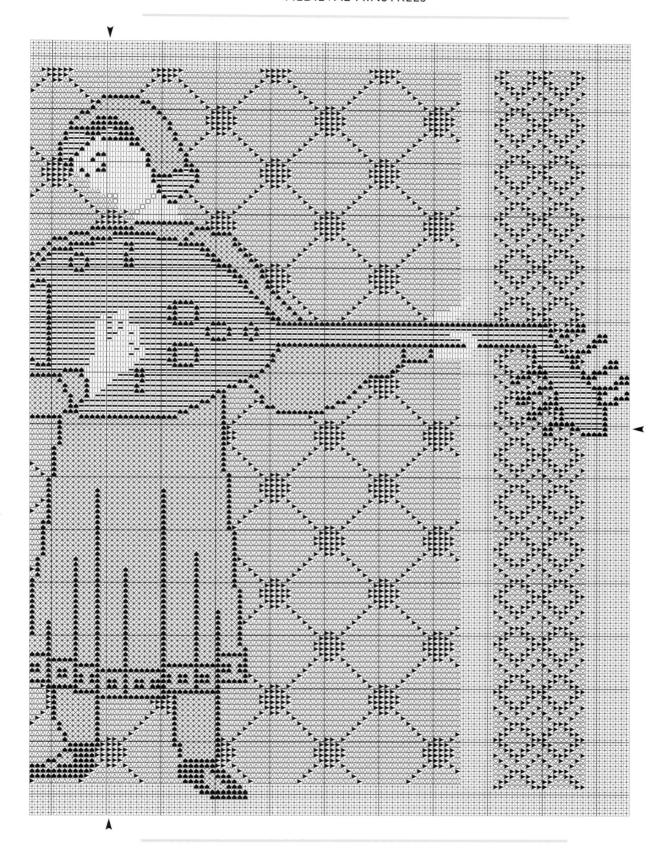

# The Cellarer

*Who could resist the charm of this cheeky cellarer,*
*sneaking a sup in secret?*

Y VERY FAVOURITE medieval design shows that there was a strong sense of humour in some of the illuminated manuscripts worked at this time. The cheeky cellarer, large bowl in hand, samples wine – and his red nose and cheeks suggest that this isn't the first time he's done so. The cellarer obviously has a very responsible position! I wonder if the artist is mocking his own kind; or is he having a dig at the corruption of the ecclesiastical orders prevalent in medieval times?

This design, in its kaleidoscope of colours, takes a minimum of 60 hours' work, but the result is well worth the effort. It isn't a simple design, and some needlepoint experience is required to complete it. The finished size in the lower-count fabrics, especially 16-count or lower, makes this an ideal design for a cushion cover.

## MATERIALS REQUIRED

- Cream congress cloth/24-count evenweave fabric, 30cm (12in) square minimum, or an appropriate size to fit on the roller frame
- 12in roller frame
- Fabric scissors and embroidery scissors
- Magnifying glass (optional)
- Tapestry needle(s) size 24
- Six-strand cotton thread:
  2 skeins of:

|  | DMC | Anchor |
|---|---|---|
| Light olive | 734 | 279 |
| Darkest brown | 3371 | 382 |

1 skein of each of:

|  | DMC | Anchor |
|---|---|---|
| Medium blue | 312 | 979 |
| Plum | 315 | 1019 |
| Salmon pink | 352 | 9 |
| Light brown | 437 | 362 |
| Light grey | 647 | 1040 |
| Light blue | 800 | 144 |
| Deep brown | 829 | 906 |
| Mid brown | 841 | 1082 |
| Dark coral | 891 | 35 |
| Flesh pink | 950 | 4146 |
| Tan | 3045 | 888 |
| Dark flesh | 3772 | 1007 |
| Yellow | 3823 | 386 |
| Rust | 3827 | 311 |
| Cream | ecru | 387 |

**STITCH COUNT:** 161 x 163

**FINISHED SIZE:**

17 x 17.3cm ($6^3/4$ x $6^7/8$in) on 24-count congress cloth

**ALTERNATIVE SCALES**

16-count: 25.6 x 25.9cm ($10^1/8$ x $10^1/4$in)
22-count: 18.6 x 18.8cm ($7^1/4$ x $7^3/8$in)
34-count: 12 x 12.2cm ($4^3/4$ x $4^7/8$in)
60-count: 6.8 x 6.9cm (approx. $2^3/4$in sq.)

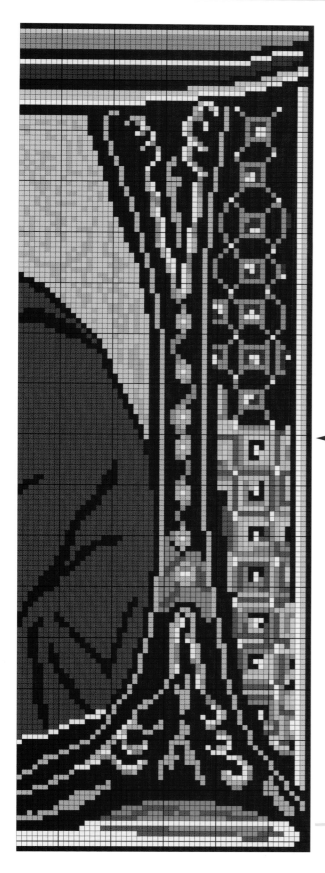

The Cellarer is a complex design that needs concentration and precision. The border is plain and can be stitched first if you prefer; if you do want to begin with the border, make sure that you get the correct number of stitches so that the central panel will fit inside it accurately. Then start in the centre of the panel with the monk, working the outlines and then filling in the details. Work out from here.

My own personal preference for this design is to stitch it diagonally from the top right-hand corner across to the bottom left-hand corner. I found this to be the easiest way to tackle this complex, highly detailed piece.

| Key | DMC | Anchor |
|---|---|---|
| Medium blue | 312 | 979 |
| Plum | 315 | 1019 |
| Salmon pink | 352 | 9 |
| Light brown | 437 | 362 |
| Light grey | 647 | 1040 |
| Light olive | 734 | 279 |
| Light blue | 800 | 144 |
| Deep brown | 829 | 906 |
| Mid brown | 841 | 1082 |
| Dark coral | 891 | 35 |
| Flesh pink | 950 | 4146 |
| Tan | 3045 | 888 |
| Darkest brown | 3371 | 382 |
| Dark flesh | 3772 | 1007 |
| Yellow | 3823 | 386 |
| Rust | 3827 | 311 |
| Cream | ecru | 387 |

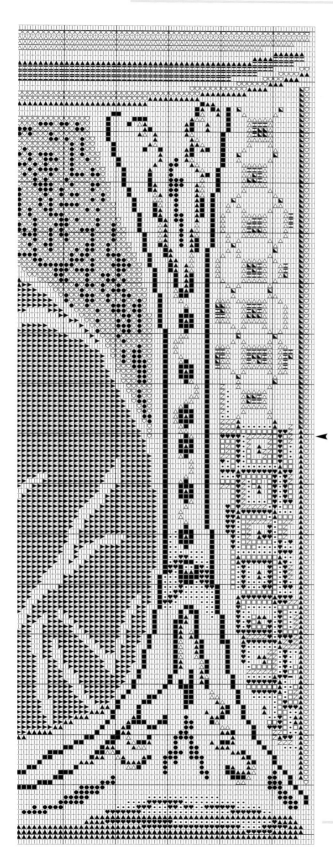

| | Key | DMC | Anchor |
|---|---|---|---|
| H | Medium blue | 312 | 979 |
| ♥ | Plum | 315 | 1019 |
| Z | Salmon pink | 352 | 9 |
| — | Light brown | 437 | 362 |
| ■ | Light grey | 647 | 1040 |
| ▽ | Light olive | 734 | 279 |
| ◤ | Light blue | 800 | 144 |
| ▶ | Deep brown | 829 | 906 |
| △ | Mid brown | 841 | 1082 |
| · | Dark coral | 891 | 35 |
| ◤ | Flesh pink | 950 | 4146 |
| ● | Tan | 3045 | 888 |
| \| | Darkest brown | 3371 | 382 |
| T | Dark flesh | 3772 | 1007 |
| ▲ | Yellow | 3823 | 386 |
| □ | Rust | 3827 | 311 |
| ✕ | Cream | ecru | 387 |

# The Teutonic Knight

*Bring back the days of chivalry with a depiction of a knight and his heraldic symbols*

**T**HE TEUTONIC ORDER OF KNIGHTS (a smaller German version of the Knights Templar and Knights Hospitaller) were originally from monastic military orders. They were a charitable order dedicated to the defence of German pilgrims, and they ran a field hospital for wounded German knights outside the city of Acre during its siege by Richard the Lionheart in 1191.

I found this image in an illuminated manuscript called the *Manesse Codex*. It shows the thirteenth-century German poet Tannhäuser in knightly garb; he belonged to the Teutonic Order of Knights. In order to be a member of the order, knights generally had to be of German knightly descent, and of legitimate birth. Highly skilled men-at-arms who were not knights, and priests, were also allowed to be members.

## MATERIALS REQUIRED

- Cream congress cloth/24-count evenweave fabric, 30cm (12in) square minimum, or an appropriate size to fit on the roller frame
- 12in roller frame
- Fabric scissors and embroidery scissors
- Magnifying glass (optional)
- Tapestry needle(s) size 24
- Six-strand cotton thread:
  1 skein of each of:

|  | DMC | Anchor |
| --- | --- | --- |
| Brown-green | 371 | 887 |
| Tan | 435 | 365 |
| Red | 498 | 1005 |
| Pale blue | 519 | 1038 |
| Beige | 613 | 831 |
| Brown | 640 | 393 |
| Dark grey | 645 | 273 |
| Mid grey | 646 | 8581 |
| Pale grey | 647 | 1040 |
| Dark tan | 780 | 309 |
| Cream | 822 | 390 |
| Mustard | 833 | 874 |
| Flesh | 945 | 881 |
| Bright green | 3347 | 266 |

**STITCH COUNT:** 115 x 158

**FINISHED SIZE:**
12.2 x 16.7cm (4$^{7}$/8 x 6$^{1}$/2in)
on 24-count congress cloth

**ALTERNATIVE SCALES**
16-count: 18.3 x 25.1cm (7$^{1}$/4 x 9$^{7}$/8in)
22-count: 13.3 x 18.2cm (5$^{1}$/4 x 7$^{1}$/8in)
34-count: 8.6 x 11.8cm (3$^{3}$/8 x 4$^{5}$/8in)
60-count: 4.9 x 6.7cm (1$^{7}$/8 x 2$^{5}$/8in)

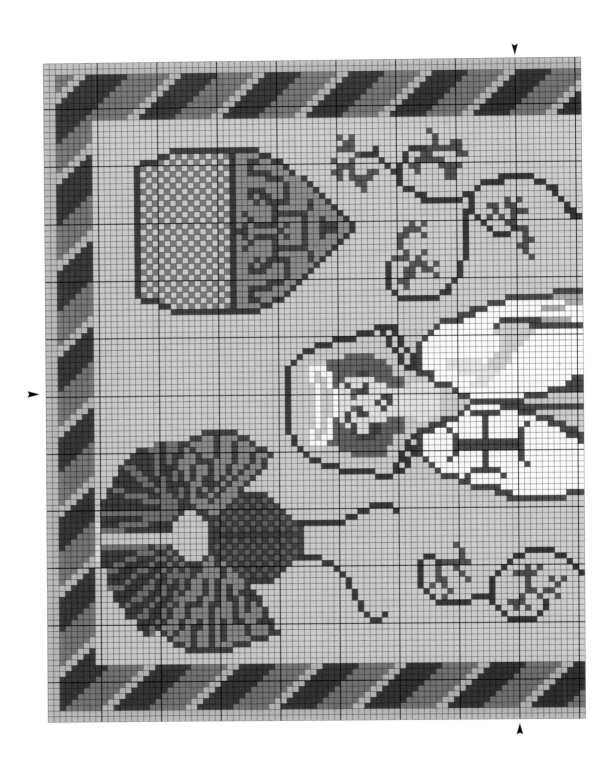

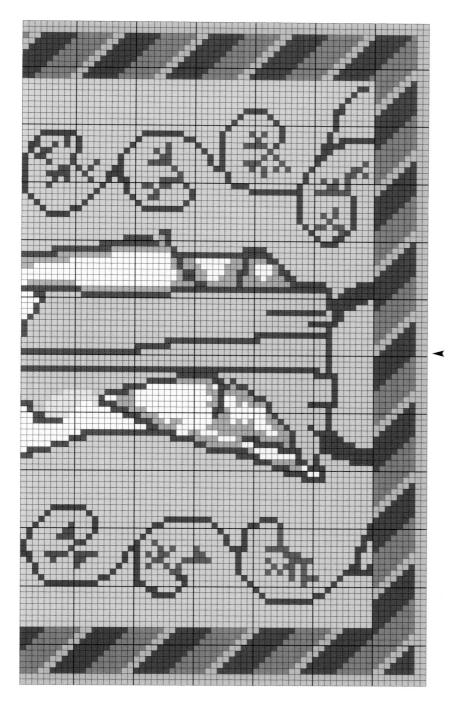

The Teutonic Knight is another easy-to-sew pattern. The design does have a regular plain border, though, so work this first; once the border is completed the rest is simple. From the centre of the design, stitch the detail of the design and the outlines of the knight. Fill these in; then, lastly, the background colour is worked. This project will take at least 40 hours' stitching.

| Key | DMC | Anchor |
|---|---|---|
| Brown-green | 371 | 887 |
| Tan | 435 | 365 |
| Red | 498 | 1005 |
| Pale blue | 519 | 1038 |
| Beige | 613 | 831 |
| Brown | 640 | 393 |
| Dark grey | 645 | 273 |
| Mid grey | 646 | 8581 |
| Pale grey | 647 | 1040 |
| Dark tan | 780 | 309 |
| Cream | 822 | 390 |
| Mustard | 833 | 874 |
| Flesh | 945 | 881 |
| Bright green | 3347 | 266 |

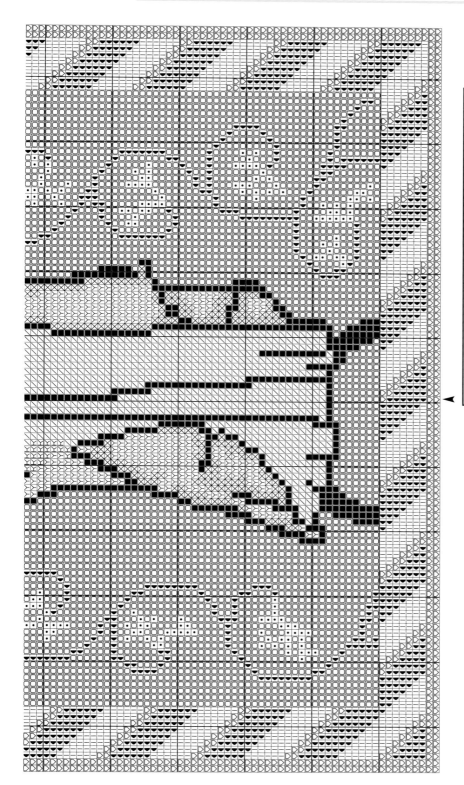

| Key | | DMC | Anchor |
|---|---|---|---|
| S | Brown-green | 371 | 887 |
| ǀ | Tan | 435 | 365 |
| ◀ | Red | 498 | 1005 |
| ╱ | Pale blue | 519 | 1038 |
| ▢ | Beige | 613 | 831 |
| ▬ | Brown | 640 | 393 |
| ■ | Dark grey | 645 | 273 |
| ♥ | Mid grey | 646 | 8581 |
| ✕ | Pale grey | 647 | 1040 |
| ▼ | Dark tan | 780 | 309 |
| Y | Cream | 822 | 390 |
| ▽ | Mustard | 833 | 874 |
| K | Flesh | 945 | 881 |
| • | Bright green | 3347 | 266 |

# The Angel on Horseback

*An angel rides out in splendour, highlighted with gold thread for extra opulence*

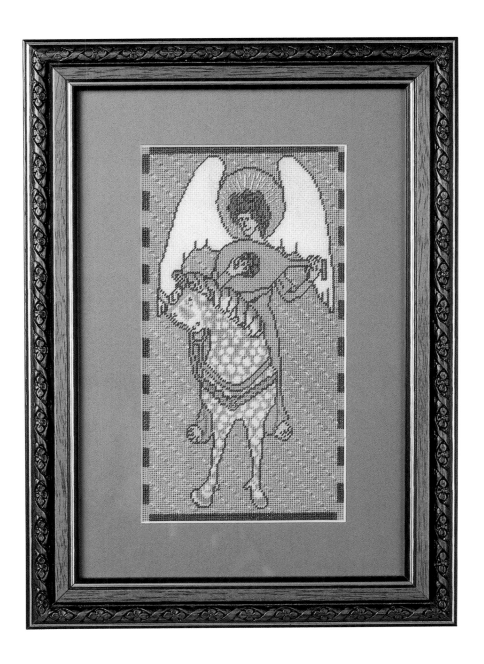

ANOTHER ONE OF my favourite designs, this angel is taken from a detailed embroidery found on the Steeple Aston Cope. A cope is a beautiful mantle worn during church ceremonies by an important cleric. The Steeple Aston Cope is an English piece dating from around 1310-40, and is worked in silk twill embroidered with silver-gilt and silver threads, and coloured silks. It's such a beautiful piece that it was later also used as an altar frontal.

The angel is just one of the many figures worked on the cope. I felt that this design should include some metallic threads to represent the opulence of the original work, and so I've used long straight stitches in metallic gold thread to highlight the design after the piece has been worked. (This detail can be omitted if you prefer.) I've marked the highlights as straight black lines on the charts.

This is a very large piece designed for a 1/12 scale room box. It's also a rather dominant piece, so I'd suggest that you use a large room box and build up your setting around the wall hanging. The design also makes a wonderful framed picture.

## MATERIALS REQUIRED

- Cream congress cloth/24-count evenweave fabric, 30cm (12in) square minimum, or an appropriate size to fit on the roller frame
- 12in roller frame
- Fabric scissors and embroidery scissors
- Magnifying glass (optional)
- Tapestry needle(s) size 24
- 1 skein of DMC stranded metallic gold thread

- Six-strand cotton thread:
  2 skeins of each of:

|  | DMC | Anchor |
|---|---|---|
| Dark mink | 640 | 393 |
| Deep brown | 898 | 380 |
| Medium grey | 3023 | 899 |

1 skein of each of:

|  | DMC | Anchor |
|---|---|---|
| Rust | 436 | 363 |
| Pale yellow | 445 | 228 |
| Grey-green | 524 | 858 |
| Light brown | 642 | 392 |
| Cream | 746 | 275 |
| Orange | 783 | 307 |
| Olive | 833 | 874 |
| Dark flesh | 950 | 4146 |

## STITCH COUNT: 106 x 192

## FINISHED SIZE:
11.2 x 20.3cm (4³/8 x 8in)
on 24-count congress cloth

## ALTERNATIVE SCALES
16-count: 16.8 x 30.5cm (6⁵/8 x 12in)
22-count: 12.2 x 22.2cm (4³/4 x 8³/4in)
34count: 7.9 x 14.3cm (3¹/8 x 5⁵/8in)
60-count: 4.5 x 8.1cm (1³/4 x 3¹/4in)

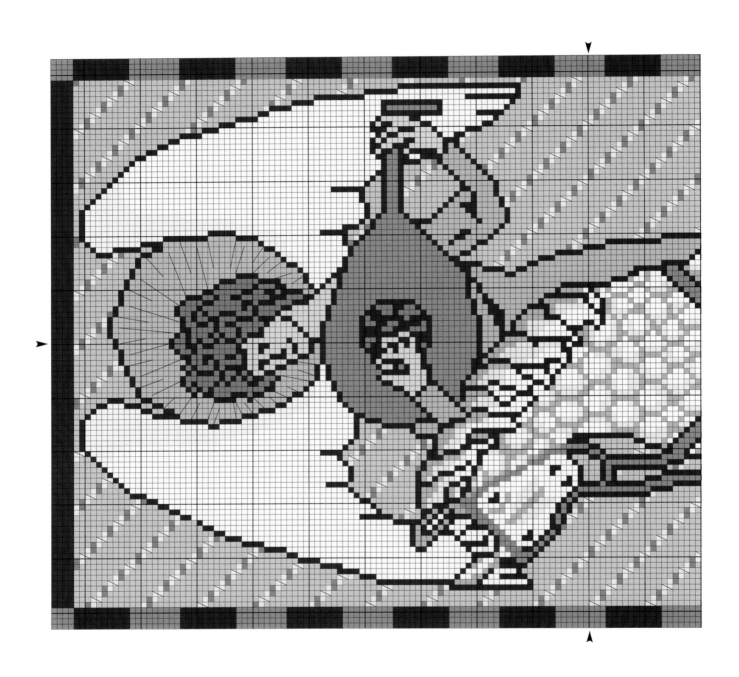

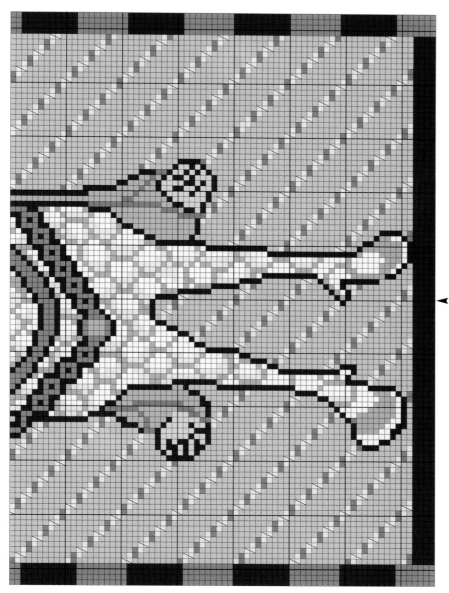

| Key | | DMC | Anchor |
|---|---|---|---|
| | Rust | 436 | 363 |
| | Pale yellow | 445 | 365 |
| | Grey-green | 524 | 858 |
| | Dark mink | 640 | 393 |
| | Light brown | 642 | 392 |
| | Cream | 746 | 275 |
| | Orange | 783 | 307 |
| | Olive | 833 | 874 |
| | Deep brown | 898 | 380 |
| | Dark flesh | 950 | 4146 |
| | Medium grey | 3023 | 899 |
| | Metallic gold thread | | |

### ∼ Stitching Tip ∼

Stitch the border design first. Then, starting in the centre of the main design, work the dappled effect of the horse. (It's important to get this area right; if you try to work the outline of the horse first, just a few stitches out of place will make a very big difference.) The outlines of the horse, angel and lute are next, then their background colours; lastly the background pattern is stitched.

Then, if you wish, add the highlights to the halo and the background to give a metallic sheen and a slightly more textured look to the design.

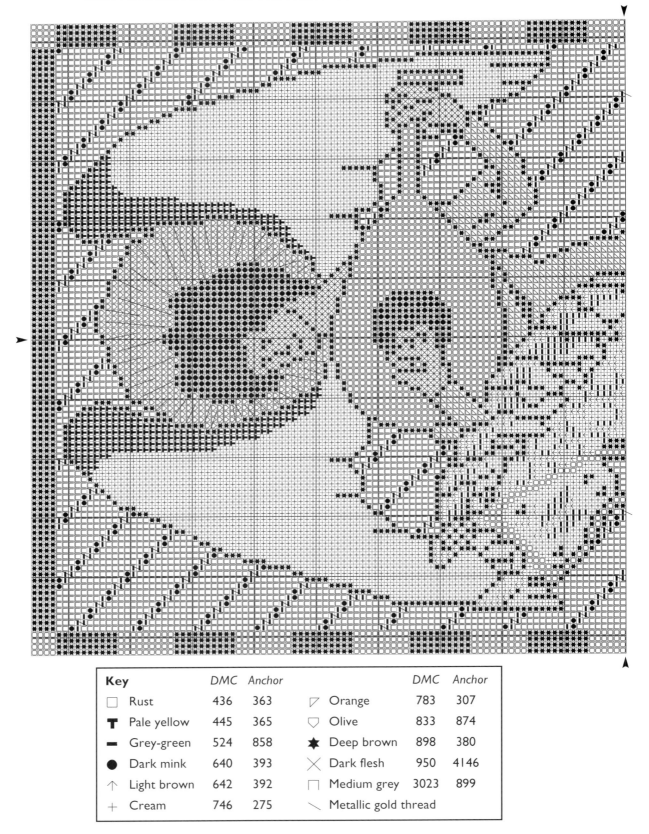

| Key | DMC | Anchor | | DMC | Anchor |
|---|---|---|---|---|---|
| ☐ Rust | 436 | 363 | ▷ Orange | 783 | 307 |
| T Pale yellow | 445 | 365 | ▽ Olive | 833 | 874 |
| — Grey-green | 524 | 858 | ★ Deep brown | 898 | 380 |
| ● Dark mink | 640 | 393 | ✕ Dark flesh | 950 | 4146 |
| ↑ Light brown | 642 | 392 | ☐ Medium grey | 3023 | 899 |
| + Cream | 746 | 275 | ＼ Metallic gold thread | | |

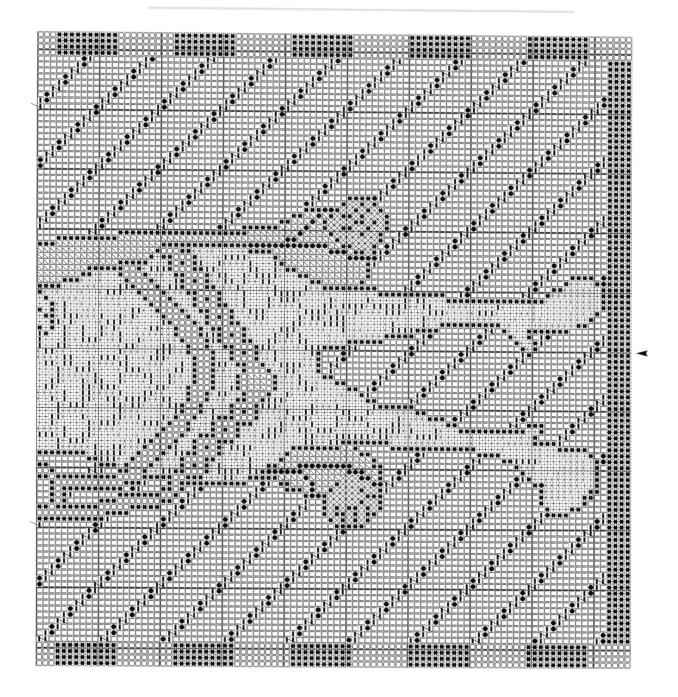

# The Hunt

*The thrill of the hunt captured in glorious coloured thread*

HE HUNT DESIGN, adapted from a fourteenth-century illustration, was one of the first designs I selected as the inspiration for a miniature wall hanging. It certainly translated well into needlepoint, and has proven to be one of my most popular designs.

The scene shows King John (King of England from 1199 to 1216) at one of his favourite pastimes. The dog races alongside the royal steed, and the slightly worried-looking stag is caught in full flight. Stylized trees at each side add a rustic feel to the scene. It seems as though John found relationships with people very difficult, much preferring the company of his animals. Several illustrations of the time show him hunting, or playing with his dogs.

As well as working successfully in miniature, this design would be useful as a wall hanging for a full-scale home. For instance, stitching the design onto 8-count canvas will create a panel measuring 51 x 38cm (20 x 15in) – quite a sizeable stitching project.

## MATERIALS REQUIRED

- Cream congress cloth/24-count evenweave fabric, 30cm (12in) square minimum, or an appropriate size to fit on the roller frame
- 12in roller frame
- Fabric scissors and embroidery scissors
- Magnifying glass (optional)
- Tapestry needle(s) size 24
- Six-strand cotton thread:
  2 skeins of:

|  | DMC | Anchor |
|---|---|---|
| Red | 349 | 13 |

1 skein of each of:

|  | DMC | Anchor |
|---|---|---|
| Dark rust | 301 | 1049 |
| Pale green | 472 | 253 |
| Mushroom | 642 | 392 |
| Grey | 647 | 1040 |
| Bright green | 702 | 226 |
| Gold | 729 | 890 |
| Blue | 791 | 178 |
| Light brown | 840 | 1084 |
| Brown | 869 | 375 |
| Dark brown | 938 | 381 |
| Flesh | 948 | 1011 |
| Cream | 3047 | 852 |
| Light rust | 3776 | 1048 |

**STITCH COUNT:** 160 x 120

**FINISHED SIZE:**
16.9 x 12.7cm (6⁵⁄8 x 5in)
on 24-count congress cloth

**ALTERNATIVE SCALES**
16-count: 25.4 x 19cm (10 x 7¹⁄2in)
22-count: 18.5 x 13.9cm (7¹⁄4 x 5¹⁄2in)
34-count: 12 x 9cm (4³⁄4 x 3¹⁄2in)
60-count: 6.8 x 5.1cm (2⁵⁄8 x 2in)

| **Key** | DMC | Anchor |
|---|---|---|
| Dark rust | 301 | 1049 |
| Red | 349 | 13 |
| Pale green | 472 | 253 |
| Mushroom | 642 | 392 |
| Grey | 647 | 1040 |
| Bright green | 702 | 226 |
| Gold | 729 | 890 |
| Blue | 791 | 178 |
| Light brown | 840 | 1084 |
| Brown | 869 | 375 |
| Dark brown | 938 | 381 |
| Flesh | 948 | 1011 |
| Cream | 3047 | 852 |
| Light rust | 3776 | 1048 |

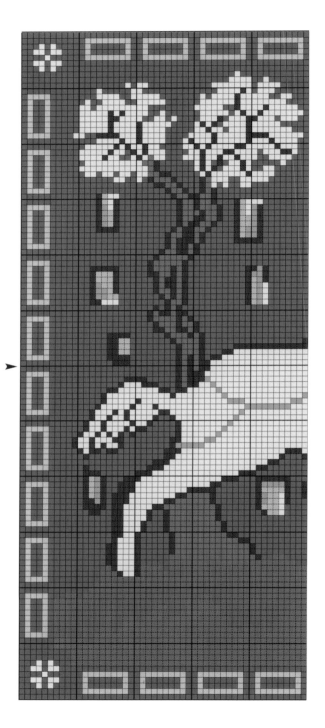

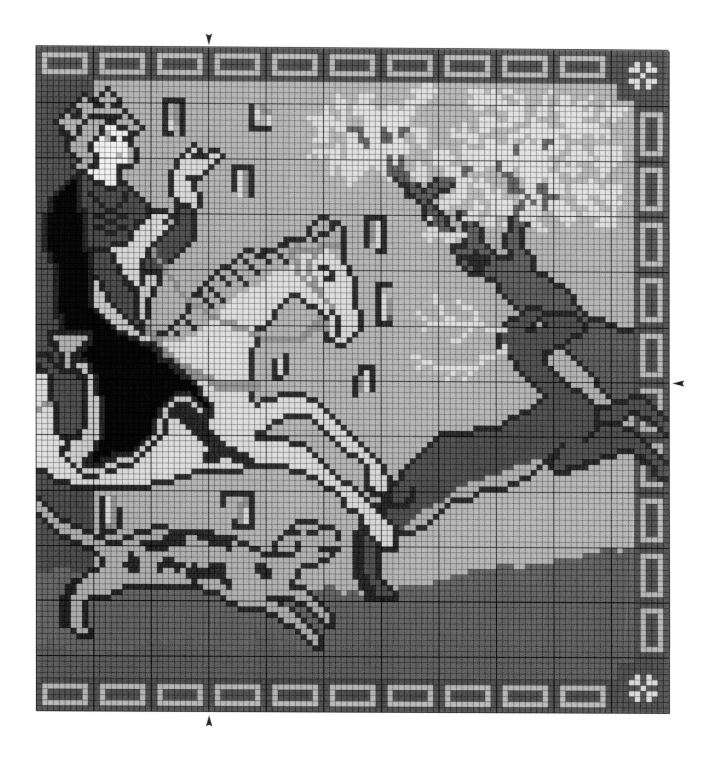

| Key | DMC | Anchor |
|---|---|---|
| ★ Dark rust | 301 | 1049 |
| • Red | 349 | 13 |
| □ Pale green | 472 | 253 |
| ▽ Mushroom | 642 | 392 |
| ● Grey | 647 | 1040 |
| S Bright green | 702 | 226 |
| ▬ Gold | 729 | 890 |
| ■ Blue | 791 | 178 |
| ◀ Light brown | 840 | 1084 |
| ☑ Brown | 869 | 375 |
| ♥ Dark brown | 938 | 381 |
| ✕ Flesh | 948 | 1011 |
| ✓ Cream | 3047 | 852 |
| △ Light rust | 3776 | 1048 |

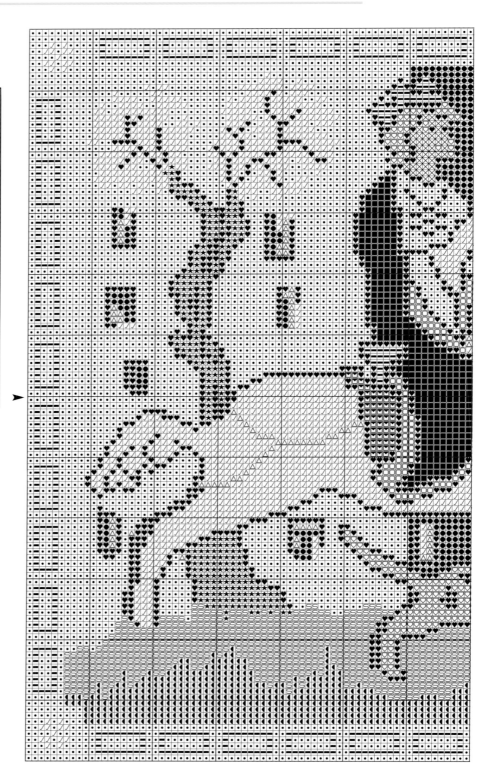

Tudor Designs

# Tudor Inspirations

*I* HAVE TO ADMIT that the Tudor period is a particular favourite of mine for several reasons. It was during the reign of Elizabeth I that tent stitch began to be used, particularly on soft furnishings, to give a 'tapestry' look to pieces. Canvaswork embroidery was actually begun during this era, and it continued to be popular until the early eighteenth century. Stitched items such as headboards or 'testers', chair-covers, screens, table carpets, cushions and hangings were worked in abundance during this period of history, and Anne Boleyn, Mary, Queen of Scots and Bess of Hardwick are just a few of the ladies whose work is still available for us to see today.

## Tudor wall hangings

Large wall hangings in the Tudor period were mainly true tapestries, woven in workshops, the majority of which were imported from Europe (particularly from Flanders and from France). Wall hangings had previously served a practical purpose, in helping to exclude draughts, but were mainly used at this time as a great status symbol and indicator of enormous wealth. These works of art were often sold as sets consisting of several pieces and were extremely costly.

Among the subjects depicted in tapestry were hunting and rural scenes, classical images and Bible stories. One fine example of Biblical scenes is the nine-piece set entitled *The History of Abraham*, bought by Henry VIII; it's one of the greatest treasures at Hampton Court today. Cardinal Wolsey had an obsession for tapestries: he purchased 21 complete sets (over 130 pieces in total) in just one month to adorn Hampton Court!

## Precious possessions

Tapestries were valuable assets, and so were looked after very carefully. During the reign of Henry VIII they were cleaned by rubbing them with bread and then brushing them to remove any residual crumbs. Far from ideal, I should think – imagine all those mouldy breadcrumbs left behind on the fabric! The tapestries were

also protected from wear by regular changing, so a vast stock of tapestries would be required in storage. Some tapestries had seasonal images specifically for this purpose.

Tapestries were often created to fit specific rooms, and then the actual furnishing of the room was designed to complement the tapestries. There were smaller hangings that were narrower strips designed to hang between two windows, and also very wide strips that were placed over doorways and above panelling. The cost of each tapestry was determined by the size and complexity of the piece, as well as by the materials used in its working; the use of metallic threads and silks substantially raised the cost.

*Above:* Hardwick Hall, the splendid residence of Bess of Hardwick, provides endless sources of inspiration for the embroiderer

## Bess of Hardwick

I'm very fortunate to live near a beautiful Tudor country house, once the home of Elizabeth (Bess) of Hardwick, Countess of Shrewsbury. Hardwick Hall is truly a goldmine for needlework enthusiasts. The hall itself, and the needlework collection that it houses, are great inspirations to any stitcher. Bess did purchase a lot of tapestries from Flanders but she was a careful housekeeper in spite of her great wealth; although the tapestries had silk highlights, almost none of them contained the metallic threads that substantially increased their cost.

# The Flower Panel

*Here's flowers for you:*
*Hot lavender, mints, savory, marjoram;*
*The marigold, that goes to bed with the sun,*
*And with him rises weeping.*
Shakespeare: *The Winter's Tale*

*I*'VE USED TYPICAL ELEMENTS of embroidery from the period to create my own design for this little flower panel. The combination of flower and animal themes was very common during Tudor times, and there were several workbooks available at this time that outlined designs for the embroiderer to use. The designs would then be copied by the embroiderer onto the canvas or linen to be sewn. Artists could also be hired to draw designs onto the fabric for the embroiderers to work on.

One typical such workbook is *A Schole-House for the Needle*, first published in 1632; a copy of this book is in the Victoria and Albert Museum, although a more complete version turned up at a jumble sale in Newport, Shropshire in the 1940s. The book contains over 60 illustrations of patterns from the sixteenth and seventeenth centuries, and is certainly the type of work from which the Tudor embroiderers and lacemakers would have taken their inspiration for designs. Facsimiles are still available today as a useful pattern source.

## MATERIALS REQUIRED

- Cream congress cloth/24-count evenweave fabric approximately 15 x 18cm (6 x 7in) minimum (or larger to fit your sewing frame)
- Frame, masking tape, drawing pins
- Fabric scissors and embroidery scissors
- Magnifying glass (optional)
- Tapestry needle(s) size 24
- Six-strand cotton thread: 1 skein of each of:

| | DMC | Anchor |
|---|---|---|
| Rose | 223 | 895 |
| Burgundy | 315 | 1019 |
| Mid pink | 316 | 1017 |
| Red | 347 | 1025 |
| Mid green | 502 | 877 |
| Pale green | 504 | 206 |
| Taupe | 613 | 831 |
| Dark brown | 898 | 380 |
| Turquoise | 930 | 1035 |
| Dark mushroom | 3032 | 898 |
| Cream | 3046 | 887 |
| Dark olive | 3051 | 845 |
| Light olive | 3052 | 844 |

**STITCH COUNT:** 81 x 112

**FINISHED SIZE:**
8.6 x 12cm (3³/8 x 4³/4in) on 24-count congress cloth

**ALTERNATIVE SCALES**
16-count: 12.9 x 17.9cm (5 x 7in)
22-count: 9.4 x 13cm (3³/4 x 5¹/8in)
34-count: 6.1 x 8.4cm (2³/8 x 3¹/4in)
60-count: 3.4 x 4.8cm (1³/8 x 1⁷/8in)

## ∾ *Stitching Tip* ∾

I work this design so that the outer border is stitched first. Work the flower and bird motifs in outline, then fill them in; lastly, work the background stitches.

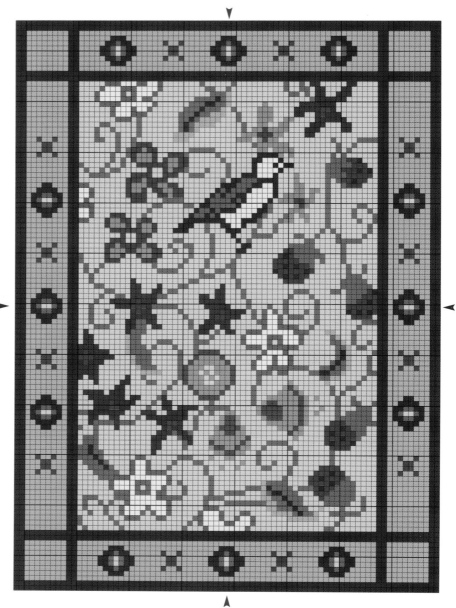

| | Key | DMC | Anchor | | | | DMC | Anchor |
|---|---|---|---|---|---|---|---|---|
| △ | Rose | 223 | 895 | ● | Dark brown | | 898 | 380 |
| ▬ | Burgundy | 315 | 1019 | ▶ | Turquoise | | 930 | 1035 |
| ○ | Mid pink | 316 | 1017 | + | Dark mushroom | | 3032 | 898 |
| ▲ | Red | 347 | 1025 | T | Cream | | 3046 | 887 |
| ■ | Mid green | 502 | 877 | ⬟ | Dark olive | | 3051 | 845 |
| ⌐ | Pale green | 504 | 206 | ▷ | Light olive | | 3052 | 844 |
| ✕ | Taupe | 613 | 831 | | | | | |

# The Elizabethan Panel

*Delicate flowers nestle inside an octagonal frame,*
*inspired by the botanical embroideries of Bess of Hardwick*

*T*HE NEEDLEWORK COLLECTION at Hardwick Hall contains a series of designs that inspired this piece – one of my favourite (and most popular) patterns. Most of the designs bear the initials ES, and are thought to have been worked by Elizabeth of Hardwick herself, using Latin inscriptions instead of the more popular mottoes. The sources for the original designs are thought to be the 1568 and 1572 editions of a book by the botanist Pietro Andrea Mattioli. As Elizabeth had a love of gardens and plants it's not surprising that some of her embroidery reflects this enthusiasm.

This design has been used on cards, dolls' house bedheads and coasters, to name but a few different items. I'm sure that you'll find a multitude of uses of your own for this small pattern.

I'm told that the lettering on this border reads 'Do not touch the crown.' I wonder if the plant is poisonous, or if this text has some more sinister meaning – probably unlikely, especially if the design was taken from a botanical source.

## MATERIALS REQUIRED

- Cream congress cloth/24-count evenweave fabric 10cm (4in) square minimum (or larger to fit your sewing frame)
- Frame, masking tape, drawing pins
- Fabric scissors and embroidery scissors
- Magnifying glass (optional)
- Tapestry needle(s) size 24
- Six-strand cotton thread:

I skein of each of:

|  | DMC | Anchor |
|---|---|---|
| Honey | 422 | 372 |
| Mid tan | 435 | 365 |
| Grey | 648 | 900 |
| Mid brown | 840 | 1084 |
| Beige | 842 | 1080 |
| Burgundy | 902 | 897 |
| Dark green | 934 | 862 |
| Mustard | 3045 | 888 |
| Olive green | 3051 | 845 |
| Light green | 3053 | 843 |

**STITCH COUNT:** 70 x 70

**FINISHED SIZE:**
7.4 x 7.4cm ($2^7/8$ x $2^7/8$in)
on 24-count congress cloth

**ALTERNATIVE SCALES**
16-count: 11.1 x 11.1cm ($4^3/8$ x $4^3/8$in)
22-count: 8.1 x 8.1cm ($3^1/8$ x $3^1/8$in)
34-count: 5.2 x 5.2cm (2 x 2in)
60-count: 3 x 3cm ($1^1/8$ x $1^1/8$in)

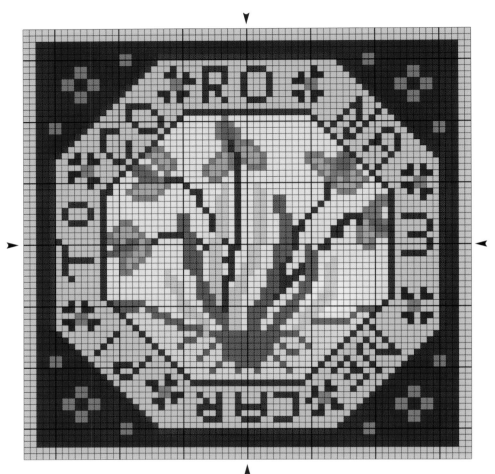

| Key | DMC | Anchor |
|---|---|---|
| Honey | 422 | 372 |
| Mid tan | 435 | 365 |
| Grey | 648 | 900 |
| Mid brown | 840 | 1084 |
| Beige | 842 | 1080 |
| Burgundy | 902 | 897 |
| Dark green | 934 | 862 |
| Mustard | 3045 | 888 |
| Olive green | 3051 | 845 |
| Light green | 3053 | 843 |

## ～ Stitching Tip ～

I stitched the border design first, then the detail, and finally the background. Make sure that you use the black and white chart as well as the colour chart to help you to identify the different greens and browns in this design correctly.

| Key | DMC | Anchor |
|---|---|---|
| ◧ Honey | 422 | 372 |
| ▬ Mid tan | 435 | 365 |
| ♡ Grey | 648 | 900 |
| ┃ Mid brown | 840 | 1084 |
| ✕ Beige | 842 | 1080 |
| ▲ Burgundy | 902 | 897 |
| ■ Dark green | 934 | 862 |
| ▢ Mustard | 3045 | 888 |
| ● Olive green | 3051 | 845 |
| ▽ Light green | 3053 | 843 |

# The Long Flower Panel

*The long proportions of this panel make it ideal for
hanging in the space between two windows*

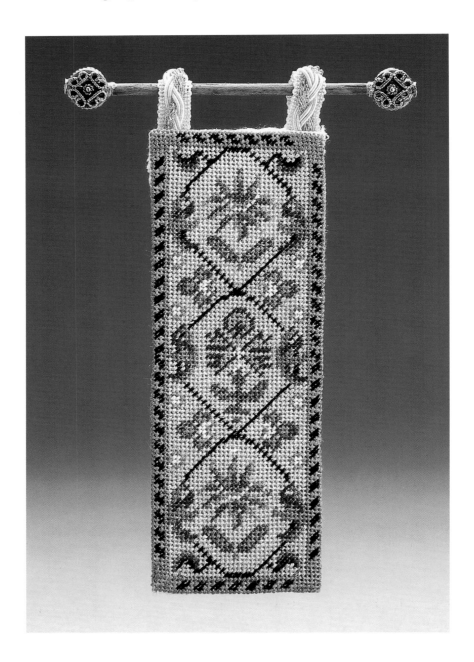

$\mathcal{J}$N THE MEDIEVAL PERIOD, long panels hung between two windows were used mainly for draught exclusion, but by Tudor times they were mainly for show. A panel such as this would be known as an *entre-fenêtre*; the phrase literally means 'in between windows'. I designed this one specially for those dolls' house enthusiasts who wanted smaller pieces for their houses.

Frequently an *entre-fenêtre* panel was designed to fit a particular wall area, although there would certainly have been occasions when a room would be designed around an existing panel – they were such costly, treasured items. Horizontal long panels were also often made to fit above panelling.

This pretty little design has a number of uses, from a bookmark to a carpet runner for late-period dolls' houses.

## MATERIALS REQUIRED

- Cream congress cloth/24-count evenweave fabric 10 x 18cm (4 x 7in) minimum (or larger to fit your sewing frame)
- Frame, masking tape, drawing pins
- Fabric scissors and embroidery scissors
- Magnifying glass (optional)
- Tapestry needle(s) size 24
- Six-strand cotton thread: 1 skein of each of:

| | DMC | Anchor |
|---|---|---|
| Deep rose | 223 | 895 |
| Black | 310 | 403 |
| Navy | 311 | 148 |
| Grey-brown | 640 | 393 |
| Light brown | 842 | 1080 |
| Mid grey-blue | 931 | 1034 |
| Pale grey-blue | 932 | 1033 |
| Mustard | 3045 | 888 |
| Olive | 3051 | 845 |
| Light olive | 3052 | 844 |
| Plum | 3740 | 872 |
| Cream | ecru | 387 |

**STITCH COUNT:** 40 x 109

**FINISHED SIZE:**
4.2 x 11.5cm (1⁵/₈ x 4¹/₂in) on 24-count congress cloth

## ALTERNATIVE SCALES
16-count: 6.4 x 17.3cm (2¹/₂ x 6³/₄in)
22-count: 4.6 x 12.6cm (1³/₄ x 5in)
34-count: 3 x 8.1cm (1¹/₈ x 3¹/₈in)
60-count: 1.7 x 4.6cm (³/₄ x 1³/₄in)

## ~ *Stitching Tip* ~

The border design needs to be
stitched first, then the flower
details and lastly the background.

| Key | DMC | Anchor |
|-----|-----|--------|
| Rose | 223 | 895 |
| Black | 310 | 403 |
| Navy | 311 | 148 |
| Grey-brown | 640 | 393 |
| Light brown | 842 | 1080 |
| Mid grey-blue | 931 | 1034 |
| Pale grey-blue | 932 | 1033 |
| Mustard | 3045 | 888 |
| Olive | 3051 | 845 |
| Light olive | 3052 | 844 |
| Plum | 3740 | 872 |
| Cream | ecru | 387 |

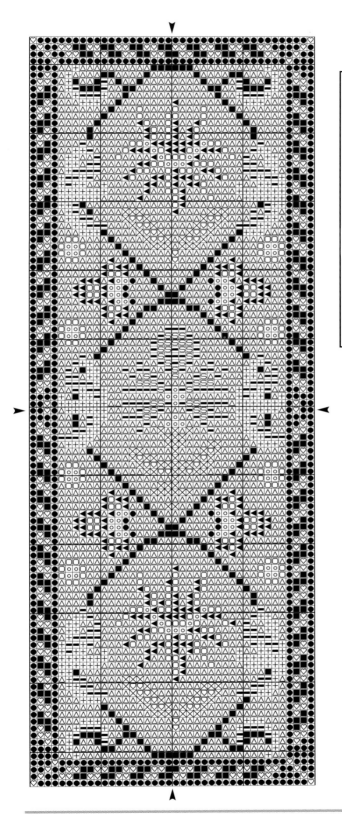

| **Key** | DMC | Anchor |
|---|---|---|
| ⬭ Rose | 223 | 895 |
| ⬛ Black | 310 | 403 |
| ▬ Navy | 311 | 148 |
| ● Grey-brown | 640 | 393 |
| △ Light brown | 842 | 1080 |
| + Mid grey-blue | 931 | 1034 |
| S Pale grey-blue | 932 | 1033 |
| ♡ Mustard | 3045 | 888 |
| ✕ Olive | 3051 | 845 |
| ▽ Light olive | 3052 | 844 |
| ◀ Plum | 3740 | 872 |
| ○ Cream | ecru | 387 |

# Elizabethan Square

*The harmony and symmetry of patterned flower beds and plants, reminiscent of a formal Elizabethan knot garden*

*T*HE TITLE IS a bit of a misnomer, as this pattern is not quite square! This design is one of my own, inspired by a cushion of coloured cutwork in the Hardwick Hall textile collection. The design is useful as a bedhead for a dolls' house, or a carpet for a later-period dolls' house; it would also make an excellent greetings card or framed picture.

Knot gardens were often depicted on textiles of the Elizabethan period. Flowers and herbs were particularly important to the Elizabethans, each plant having some special property – curative, mystical, cosmetic or culinary. I'm certain that some of the cutwork of the time, such as the piece that inspired this project, was based on the beauty and symmetry of the knot garden.

## MATERIALS REQUIRED

- Cream congress cloth/24-count evenweave fabric 15cm (6in) square minimum (or larger to fit your sewing frame)
- Frame, masking tape, drawing pins
- Fabric scissors and embroidery scissors
- Magnifying glass (optional)

- Tapestry needle(s) size 24
- Six-strand cotton thread: I skein of each of:

|  | DMC | Anchor |
|---|---|---|
| Deep rose | 223 | 895 |
| Purple | 550 | 101 |
| Beige | 613 | 831 |
| Dark green | 924 | 851 |
| Coral | 3328 | 1024 |

## STITCH COUNT: 80 x 85

## FINISHED SIZE:

8.5 x 9cm (3$^3$/8 x 3$^1$/2in) on 24-count congress cloth

## ALTERNATIVE SCALES

16-count: 12.7 x 13.5cm (5 x 5$^1$/4in)
22-count: 9.2 x 9.8cm (3$^5$/8 x 3$^7$/8in)
34-count: 6 x 6.4cm (2$^3$/8 x 2$^1$/2in)
60-count: 3.4 x 3.6cm (1$^1$/4 x 1$^3$/8in)

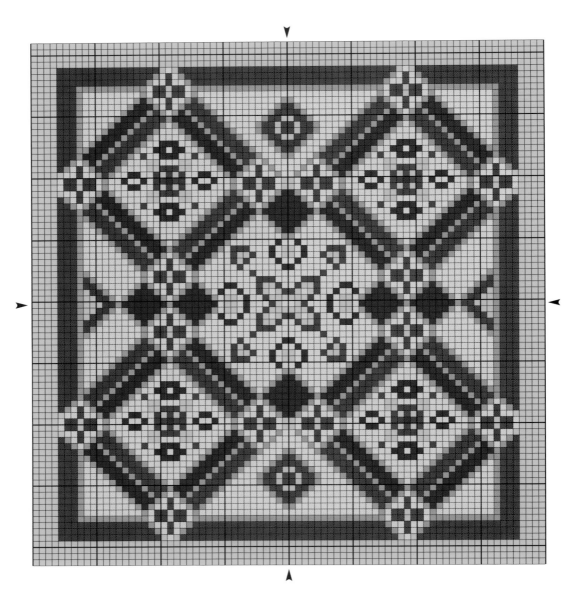

## ～ *Stitching Tip* ～

Stitching this design is straightforward.
As with some of the other designs, start
with the border. Work the inner outlines,
then the details of the pattern, and
finally the background areas.

| Key A | DMC | Anchor |
|---|---|---|
| Deep rose | 223 | 895 |
| Purple | 550 | 101 |
| Beige | 613 | 831 |
| Dark green | 924 | 851 |
| Coral | 3328 | 1024 |

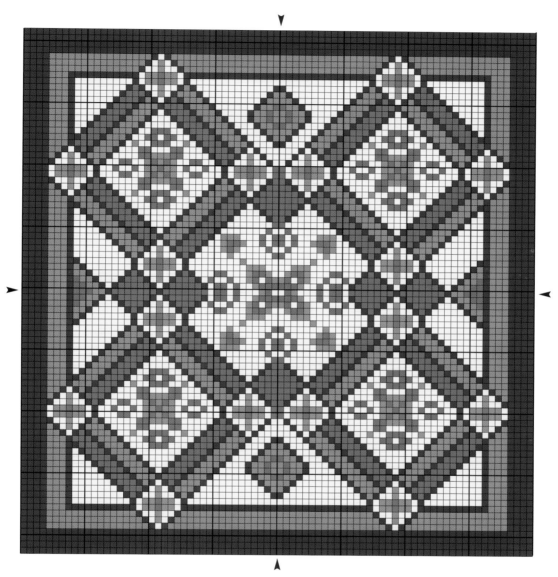

The balance of the design alters intriguingly if you choose different colours; try this colour scheme (**B**) of blues, plum and ginger. You'll need one skein of each colour in the key.

| **Key B** | DMC | Anchor |
|---|---|---|
| Blue | 312 | 979 |
| Cream | 677 | 361 |
| Navy | 823 | 152 |
| Plum | 3740 | 872 |
| Ginger | 3776 | 1048 |

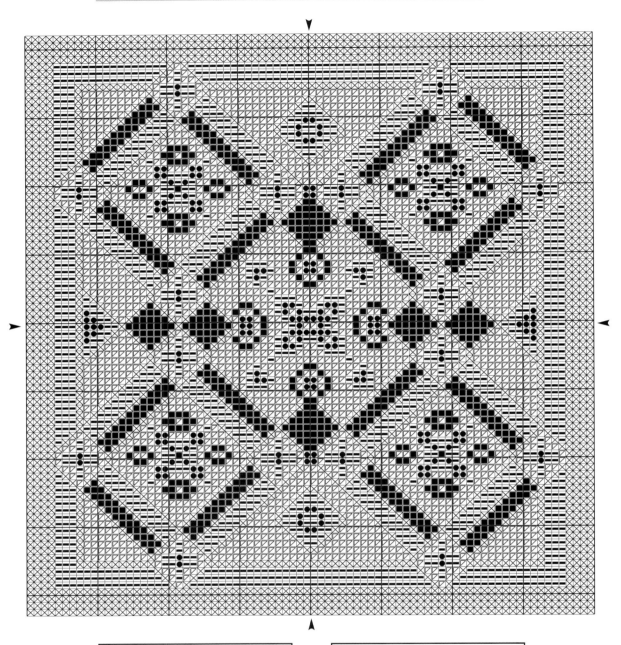

| **Key A** | DMC | Anchor |
|---|---|---|
| ● Deep rose | 223 | 895 |
| ■ Purple | 550 | 101 |
| ▽ Beige | 613 | 831 |
| — Dark green | 924 | 851 |
| ✕ Coral | 3328 | 1024 |

| **Key B** | DMC | Anchor |
|---|---|---|
| ■ Blue | 312 | 979 |
| ▽ Cream | 677 | 361 |
| ✕ Navy | 823 | 152 |
| ● Plum | 3740 | 872 |
| — Ginger | 3776 | 1048 |

# Hardwick Hall

*Stitch a peaceful garden scene, with a stylized*
*Hardwick Hall in the background, to fix your dolls'*
*house firmly in the Tudor period*

*I*NSPIRED BY the Derbyshire home of Elizabeth (Bess) of Hardwick, this is a fairly modern interpretation of the garden. As I mentioned in the introduction to this section, Hardwick Hall has been the inspiration for many of my Tudor needlepoint designs. The house is now in the hands of the National Trust, and has a remarkable exhibition of needlework dating from the time of Mary, Queen of Scots. Many of the pieces are supposed to have been sewn by Bess and Mary, when Mary was in the custody of Elizabeth's husband, George Talbot, 6th Earl of Shrewsbury, from 1568.

The actual garden at Hardwick has never been particularly elaborate; Bess needed most of her money for the house itself, and also for the refurbishment of nearby Chatsworth. This meant that little attention was paid to the grounds at Hardwick, and the garden must have had a bit of a rustic feel to it; even the grass was allowed to grow long for hay. Most of the ornamental gardening wasn't done until the nineteenth and early twentieth centuries, although some of the layout was undertaken in the seventeenth century. The garden was kept very simple, with a typical symmetrical design. The large herb garden wasn't created until the 1960s, although there is a record of a well-stocked and maintained kitchen garden in Bess's day.

The design may look detailed, but if you make a stitching mistake while you're working it, no-one would ever know!

## MATERIALS REQUIRED

- Cream congress cloth/24-count evenweave fabric 20 x 15cm (8 x 6in) minimum (or larger to fit your sewing frame)
- Frame, masking tape, drawing pins
- Fabric scissors and embroidery scissors
- Magnifying glass (optional)
- Tapestry needle(s) size 24
- Six-strand cotton thread:
  2 skeins of:

|  | DMC | Anchor |
|---|---|---|
| White | blanc | I |

I skein of each of:

|  | DMC | Anchor |
|---|---|---|
| Blue | 312 | 979 |
| Mid grey | 414 | 235 |
| Mid tan | 436 | 363 |
| Deep green | 500 | 683 |
| Sea green | 501 | 878 |
| Dark grey | 535 | 401 |
| Olive | 581 | 281 |
| Cream | 739 | 366 |
| Light blue | 800 | 144 |
| Green-brown | 829 | 906 |
| Mid brown | 869 | 375 |
| Mushroom | 3032 | 898 |
| Light green | 3053 | 843 |
| Dark pink | 3726 | 1018 |
| Emerald | 3818 | 923 |

| Key | | DMC | Anchor |
|---|---|---|---|
| | Blue | 312 | 979 |
| | Mid grey | 414 | 235 |
| | Mid tan | 436 | 363 |
| | Deep green | 500 | 683 |
| | Sea green | 501 | 878 |
| | Dark grey | 535 | 401 |
| | Olive | 581 | 281 |
| | Cream | 739 | 366 |
| | Light blue | 800 | 144 |
| | Green-brown | 829 | 906 |
| | Mid brown | 869 | 375 |
| | Mushroom | 3032 | 898 |
| | Light green | 3053 | 843 |
| | Dark pink | 3726 | 1018 |
| | Emerald | 3818 | 923 |
| | White | blanc | 1 |

∼ *Stitching Tip* ∼

Work the border design first as it has a regular stitch pattern. After this I suggest that you start in the centre and work out, working the detail and background as you go. Leave the sky until last.

**STITCH COUNT:** 88 × 128

**FINISHED SIZE:**
9.3 x 13.5cm (3⁵/8 x 5¹/4in) on 24-count congress cloth

**ALTERNATIVE SCALES**
16-count: 14 x 20.3cm (5¹/2 x 8in)
22-count: 10.2 x 14.8cm (4 x 5⁷/8in)
34-count: 6.6 x 9.6cm (2⁵/8 x 3³/4in)
60-count: 3.7 x 5.4cm (1¹/2 x 2¹/8in)

| Key | DMC | Anchor |
|---|---|---|
| ♡ Blue | 312 | 979 |
| ✕ Mid grey | 414 | 235 |
| ☐ Mid tan | 436 | 363 |
| ♥ Deep green | 500 | 683 |
| ▬ Sea green | 501 | 878 |
| ◤ Dark grey | 535 | 401 |
| + Olive | 581 | 281 |
| ♥ Cream | 739 | 366 |
| │ Light blue | 800 | 144 |
| ▶ Green-brown | 829 | 906 |
| ◀ Mid brown | 869 | 375 |
| ⼍ Mushroom | 3032 | 898 |
| ▽ Light green | 3053 | 843 |
| ╱ Dark pink | 3726 | 1018 |
| ● Emerald | 3818 | 923 |
| ∧ White | blanc | 1 |

# About the Author

SANDRA WHITEHEAD IS MARRIED, with five daughters ranging in age from 3 to 18. She lives in Grassmoor, a small mining village near Chesterfield in Derbyshire, within easy reach of the Peak District National Park.

Sandra believes that it was fate that forced her to retire early because of a back injury. Until then she'd been a Senior Lecturer in Diagnostic Radiography at Sheffield Hallam University, but retirement enabled her to fulfil her lifelong ambition to design needlework.

Her home is taken over by books, books and more books. She has a large library of history, art, dolls' house and miniatures, historical costume, textile and needlework books accumulated over many years. Reading, photography and visiting National Trust properties are her other main interests.

When she's not reading, designing or sewing she's also trying to research her family history. She set up Knight Time Miniatures in 1998, designing wall hangings for the dolls' house market. By 1999 she had enough designs to consider having them published, and this book is the result, showing the fruits of her new career.

## MADEIRA THREAD EQUIVALENTS

The numbers in the left-hand column show the DMC threads used in the projects; the right-hand column shows the nearest equivalents in the Madeira range of threads

| DMC | Madeira | DMC | Madeira | DMC | Madeira | DMC | Madeira | DMC | Madeira | DMC | Madeira | DMC | Madeira |
|---|---|---|---|---|---|---|---|---|---|---|---|---|---|
| blanc | 2402 | 414 | 1801 | 524 | 1511 | 712 | 2101 | 817 | 0211 | 928 | 1709 | 3052 | 1509 |
| ecru | 2404 | 422 | 2102 | 535 | 1809 | 729 | 2209 | 822 | 1908 | 930 | 1712 | 3053 | 1510 |
| | | 434 | 2009 | 550 | 0714 | 734 | 1610 | 823 | 1008 | 931 | 1711 | 3328 | 0406 |
| 223 | 0812 | 435 | 2010 | 581 | 1609 | 739 | 2014 | 825 | 1011 | 932 | 1710 | 3347 | 1408 |
| | | 436 | 2011 | 597 | 1110 | 744 | 0112 | 828 | 1014 | 934 | 1506 | 3371 | 2004 |
| 301 | 2306 | 437 | 2012 | | | 747 | 1104 | 829 | 2113 | 938 | 2005 | 3722 | 0812 |
| 310 | 2400 | 445 | 0103 | 640 | 1905 | 762 | 1804 | 833 | 2203 | 945 | 2309 | 3726 | 0810 |
| 311 | 1006 | 471 | 1501 | 642 | 1906 | 780 | 2214 | 838 | 2005 | 948 | 0306 | 3740 | 2614 |
| 312 | 1005 | 472 | 1414 | 644 | 1814 | 781 | 2213 | 840 | 1912 | 958 | 1114 | 3772 | 2312 |
| 315 | 0810 | 498 | 0511 | 645 | 1811 | 782 | 2213 | 841 | 1911 | 966 | 1209 | 3774 | 0306 |
| 316 | 0809 | | | 646 | 1812 | 782 | 2212 | 842 | 1910 | 971 | 0203 | 3776 | 2302 |
| 321 | 0510 | 500 | 1705 | 647 | 1813 | 783 | 2211 | 869 | 2105 | 972 | 0107 | 3808 | 2507 |
| 333 | 0903 | 501 | 1704 | 648 | 1814 | 791 | 0904 | 891 | 0411 | | | 3813 | 1701 |
| 341 | 0901 | 502 | 1703 | 677 | 2207 | 792 | 0905 | 898 | 2006 | 3023 | 1902 | 3818 | 2704 |
| 347 | 0407 | 503 | 1702 | 699 | 1303 | 796 | 0913 | | | 3032 | 2002 | 3823 | 2511 |
| 349 | 0212 | 504 | 1701 | | | 797 | 0912 | 902 | 0601 | 3045 | 2103 | 3827 | 2301 |
| 352 | 0303 | 518 | 1106 | 700 | 1304 | | | 921 | 0311 | 3046 | 2206 | | |
| 371 | 2111 | 519 | 1105 | 701 | 1305 | 800 | 0908 | 922 | 0310 | 3047 | 2205 | | |
| | | 522 | 1513 | 702 | 1306 | 815 | 0513 | 924 | 1706 | 3051 | 1508 | | |

# Index

# GMC Publications

## BOOKS

## CRAFTS

| | |
|---|---|
| American Patchwork Designs in Needlepoint | *Melanie Tacon* |
| A Beginners' Guide to Rubber Stamping | *Brenda Hunt* |
| Blackwork: A New Approach | *Brenda Day* |
| Celtic Cross Stitch Designs | *Carol Phillipson* |
| Celtic Knotwork Designs | *Sheila Sturrock* |
| Celtic Knotwork Handbook | *Sheila Sturrock* |
| Celtic Spirals and Other Designs | *Sheila Sturrock* |
| Collage from Seeds, Leaves and Flowers | *Joan Carver* |
| Complete Pyrography | *Stephen Poole* |
| Contemporary Smocking | *Dorothea Hall* |
| Creating Colour with Dylon | *Dylon International* |
| Creative Doughcraft | *Patricia Hughes* |
| Creative Embroidery Techniques Using Colour Through Gold | |
| | *Daphne J. Ashby & Jackie Woolsey* |
| The Creative Quilter: Techniques and Projects | *Pauline Brown* |
| Decorative Beaded Purses | *Enid Taylor* |
| Designing and Making Cards | *Glennis Gilruth* |
| Glass Engraving Pattern Book | *John Everett* |
| Glass Painting | *Emma Sedman* |
| Handcrafted Rugs | *Sandra Hardy* |
| How to Arrange Flowers: A Japanese Approach to English Design | |
| | *Taeko Marvelly* |
| How to Make First-Class Cards | *Debbie Brown* |
| An Introduction to Crewel Embroidery | *Mave Glenny* |
| Making and Using Working Drawings for Realistic Model Animals | |
| | *Basil F. Fordham* |
| Making Character Bears | *Valerie Tyler* |
| Making Decorative Screens | *Amanda Howes* |
| Making Fairies and Fantastical Creatures | *Julie Sharp* |
| Making Greetings Cards for Beginners | *Pat Sutherland* |
| Making Hand-Sewn Boxes: Techniques and Projects | |
| | *Jackie Woolsey* |
| Making Knitwear Fit | *Pat Ashforth & Steve Plummer* |
| Making Mini Cards, Gift Tags & Invitations | *Glennis Gilruth* |
| Making Soft-Bodied Dough Characters | *Patricia Hughes* |
| Natural Ideas for Christmas: Fantastic Decorations to Make | |
| | *Josie Cameron-Ashcroft & Carol Cox* |
| Needlepoint: A Foundation Course | *Sandra Hardy* |
| New Ideas for Crochet: Stylish Projects for the Home | |
| | *Darsha Capaldi* |
| Patchwork for Beginners | *Pauline Brown* |
| Pyrography Designs | *Norma Gregory* |
| Pyrography Handbook (Practical Crafts) | *Stephen Poole* |
| Ribbons and Roses | *Lee Lockheed* |
| Rose Windows for Quilters | *Angela Besley* |
| Rubber Stamping with Other Crafts | *Lynne Garner* |
| Sponge Painting | *Ann Rooney* |
| Stained Glass: Techniques and Projects | *Mary Shanahan* |
| Step-by-Step Pyrography Projects for the Solid Point Machine | |
| | *Norma Gregory* |
| Tassel Making for Beginners | *Enid Taylor* |
| Tatting Collage | *Lindsay Rogers* |
| Temari: A Traditional Japanese Embroidery Technique | |
| | *Margaret Ludlow* |
| Theatre Models in Paper and Card | *Robert Burgess* |
| Trip Around the World: 25 Patchwork, Quilting and Appliqué Projects | *Gail Lawther* |
| Trompe l'Oeil: Techniques and Projects | *Jan Lee Johnson* |
| Wool Embroidery and Design | *Lee Lockheed* |

## DOLLS' HOUSES AND MINIATURES

| | |
|---|---|
| 1/12 Scale Character Figures for the Dolls' House | |
| | *James Carrington* |
| Architecture for Dolls' Houses | *Joyce Percival* |
| The Authentic Georgian Dolls' House | *Brian Long* |
| A Beginners' Guide to the Dolls' House Hobby | *Jean Nisbett* |
| Celtic, Medieval and Tudor Wall Hangings in 1/12 Scale Needlepoint | *Sandra Whitehead* |
| The Complete Dolls' House Book | *Jean Nisbett* |
| The Dolls' House 1/24 Scale: A Complete Introduction | |
| | *Jean Nisbett* |
| Dolls' House Accessories, Fixtures and Fittings | *Andrea Barham* |
| Dolls' House Bathrooms: Lots of Little Loos | *Patricia King* |
| Dolls' House Fireplaces and Stoves | *Patricia King* |
| Dolls' House Window Treatments | *Eve Harwood* |
| Easy to Make Dolls' House Accessories | *Andrea Barham* |
| Heraldic Miniature Knights | *Peter Greenhill* |
| How to Make Your Dolls' House Special: Fresh Ideas for Decorating | *Beryl Armstrong* |
| Make Your Own Dolls' House Furniture | *Maurice Harper* |
| Making Dolls' House Furniture | *Patricia King* |
| Making Georgian Dolls' Houses | *Derek Rowbottom* |
| Making Miniature Food and Market Stalls | *Angie Scarr* |
| Making Miniature Gardens | *Freida Gray* |
| Making Miniature Oriental Rugs & Carpets | |
| | *Meik & Ian McNaughton* |
| Making Period Dolls' House Accessories | *Andrea Barham* |
| Making Tudor Dolls' Houses | *Derek Rowbottom* |
| Making Victorian Dolls' House Furniture | *Patricia King* |
| Miniature Bobbin Lace | *Roz Snowden* |

| Woodturning: An Individual Approach | Dave Regester |
| Woodturning: A Source Book of Shapes | John Hunnex |
| Woodturning Jewellery | Hilary Bowen |
| Woodturning Masterclass | Tony Boase |
| Woodturning Techniques | GMC Publications |
| Woodturning Tools & Equipment Test Reports | GMC Publications |
| Woodturning Wizardry | David Springett |

## WOODWORKING

| Advanced Scrollsaw Projects | GMC Publications |
| Bird Boxes and Feeders for the Garden | Dave Mackenzie |
| Complete Woodfinishing | Ian Hosker |
| David Charlesworth's Furniture-Making Techniques | |
| | David Charlesworth |
| The Encyclopedia of Joint Making | Terrie Noll |
| Furniture & Cabinetmaking Projects | GMC Publications |
| Furniture-Making Projects for the Wood Craftsman | |
| | GMC Publications |
| Furniture-Making Techniques for the Wood Craftsman | |
| | GMC Publications |
| Furniture Projects | Rod Wales |
| Furniture Restoration (Practical Crafts) | Kevin Jan Bonner |
| Furniture Restoration and Repair for Beginners | |
| | Kevin Jan Bonner |
| Furniture Restoration Workshop | Kevin Jan Bonner |
| Green Woodwork | Mike Abbott |
| Kevin Ley's Furniture Projects | Kevin Ley |
| Making & Modifying Woodworking Tools | Jim Kingshott |
| Making Chairs and Tables | GMC Publications |
| Making Classic English Furniture | Paul Richardson |
| Making Little Boxes from Wood | John Bennett |
| Making Screw Threads in Wood | Fred Holder |
| Making Shaker Furniture | Barry Jackson |
| Making Woodwork Aids and Devices | Robert Wearing |
| Mastering the Router | Ron Fox |
| Minidrill: Fifteen Projects | John Everett |
| Pine Furniture Projects for the Home | Dave Mackenzie |
| Practical Scrollsaw Patterns | John Everett |
| Router Magic: Jigs, Fixtures and Tricks to Unleash your Router's Full Potential | Bill Hylton |
| Routing for Beginners | Anthony Bailey |
| The Scrollsaw: Twenty Projects | John Everett |
| Sharpening: The Complete Guide | Jim Kingshott |
| Sharpening Pocket Reference Book | Jim Kingshott |
| Simple Scrollsaw Projects | GMC Publications |
| Space-Saving Furniture Projects | Dave Mackenzie |
| Stickmaking: A Complete Course | Andrew Jones & Clive George |
| Stickmaking Handbook | Andrew Jones & Clive George |
| Test Reports: The Router and Furniture & Cabinetmaking | |
| | GMC Publications |
| Veneering: A Complete Course | Ian Hosker |
| Veneering Handbook | Ian Hosker |
| Woodfinishing Handbook (Practical Crafts) | Ian Hosker |
| Woodworking with the Router: Professional Router Techniques any Woodworker can Use | Bill Hylton & Fred Matlack |
| The Workshop | Jim Kingshott |

## VIDEOS

| Drop-in and Pinstuffed Seats | David James |
| Stuffover Upholstery | David James |
| Elliptical Turning | David Springett |
| Woodturning Wizardry | David Springett |
| Turning Between Centres: The Basics | Dennis White |
| Turning Bowls | Dennis White |
| Boxes, Goblets and Screw Threads | Dennis White |
| Novelties and Projects | Dennis White |
| Classic Profiles | Dennis White |
| Twists and Advanced Turning | Dennis White |
| Sharpening the Professional Way | Jim Kingshott |
| Sharpening Turning & Carving Tools | Jim Kingshott |
| Bowl Turning | John Jordan |
| Hollow Turning | John Jordan |
| Woodturning: A Foundation Course | Keith Rowley |
| Carving a Figure: The Female Form | Ray Gonzalez |
| The Router: A Beginner's Guide | Alan Goodsell |
| The Scroll Saw: A Beginner's Guide | John Burke |

## MAGAZINES

WOODTURNING ◆ WOODCARVING
FURNITURE & CABINETMAKING
THE ROUTER ◆ WOODWORKING
THE DOLLS' HOUSE MAGAZINE
WATER GARDENING ◆ EXOTIC GARDENING
GARDEN CALENDAR
OUTDOOR PHOTOGRAPHY
BLACK & WHITE PHOTOGRAPHY
BUSINESSMATTERS

The above represents a full list of all titles currently published or scheduled to be published.
All are available direct from the Publishers or through bookshops, newsagents and specialist retailers.
To place an order, or to obtain a complete catalogue, contact:

**GMC Publications,
Castle Place, 166 High Street, Lewes,
East Sussex BN7 1XU, United Kingdom
Tel: 01273 488005  Fax: 01273 478606
E-mail: pubs@thegmcgroup.com**

Orders by credit card are accepted